# Metamorphosis of a Soul

## Melissa Overmyer

Dedicated to
The Blessed Virgin Mary who is Mother to us all;
to the Holy Father, Pope Francis, who makes
Catholicism look so cool;
to all of the Father Michaels of the world who love
Christ first and foremost, and humbly direct others
to find Him for themselves in the Eucharist;
and to my adorable husband and children
whom I love with all of my heart.

# Table of Contents:

"Everyone thinks of changing the world, but no one thinks of changing himself."

Leo Tolstoy

Metamorphosis (meta-mor-phoses)
Definition
a: A change of physical form, structure or substance especially by supernatural means
b: a striking alteration in appearance, character, or circumstances
www.miriam -webster.com

Soul (sol)
Definition
a: the immaterial essence, animating principle, or actuating cause of an individual life
b: a person's total self
www.miriam-webster.com

If it had not happened to me, I would be hard pressed to believe that what I am about to tell you is true. But it did all happen to me, and not just for me—as things never happen for just one individual—but for the whole body. I pray that, as you read about the metamorphoses that have taken place in my soul, that first and foremost it will bring great Glory to the One Who makes it happen, for He always knows what He is doing and for what purpose, even if we do not. And secondly, that you will recognize in your own metamorphosis the work of the Lord and join me in praising Him as we are transformed by His Grace into the new and beautiful creatures we were always intended to be.

9

As I began the journey you are about to read, I kept a journal. In it, I wrote my prayers, reflections on scripture, my questions, my fears, my doubts, the answers I was given, and even doodled pictures that I felt helped to explain all the Lord was showing to me. I am a very visual learner. At the end of each chapter is written a Praise, a Prayer, a Promise (a scripture verse) and Proof of the Promise (a bottom line take-away) and then there is an area for you to "Ponder"— to journal about your own story. If you choose to do this, it can be kept just for yourself, or you may want to share it with a friend/s or even a priest or pastor. What ever you do, I pray that the eyes of your heart will be enlightened and you will go further and deeper with our amazing and loving Lord, because we can never come to the end of Him.

## Chapter 1

*"All the way to heaven...is heaven."* --St. Teresa of Avila

*The spiritual journey begins long before we are even aware of it, for we are not the initiators of it. As much as we like to think that we are in charge of all of our life, the truth is, we are really just responding to moments of grace that God places before us. Along the road, we may receive moments of clarity called conversions that lead to transformation. About what do we suddenly see more clearly? We see and we experience Love. It's as if the Lord is tapping our shoulder saying, "Here I am. Come follow Me." And miraculously, by His grace, we do...*

**The Wake Up Call**

I am not sure if it was the spectacular, grand-finale ending of a ten-day fast, or the crashing upon my mind and heart of all he had said in the Catechism class that had me just this side of utterly deflated—or a combination of both. But what happened next could not have been more unexpected.

There she was. As beautiful and sparkly-eyed as a seventeen-year-old Mother of God could be. I knew who she was immediately by her smile—her kind and gentle gaze into my heart, into my doubts and fears. Her knowing that I was feeling distraught at the prospect of never fully becoming all I hoped to be— all because of her—all because of what he had said I must believe about her and, in my mind, I knew I could not at this time accept. And yet, she came to me anyway.

And what she spoke to me… how humble, how astonishing…the very core of truth.
If I were making this up, I would have imagined a much more bucolic setting—a beautiful garden, a mountainside, a grassy river bank, a forest trail, really just about anywhere but where I was—on a busy road, on a less than glamorous stretch of strip-mall-lined suburban commercial wasteland. But it was where she chose to be with me, in my everyday trek to the grocery store to buy in bulk what I had for ten days denied myself in order to gain clarity. And clarity is what she delivered.

As I drove, I re-hashed the words I'd heard in the class...*Immaculate Conception, Ever Virgin, without sin.* My formerly Baptist brain, though having already been stretched into a more sacramentally receptive vessel, was now being asked to contort into a new realm of open-mindedness. Mental and spiritual gymnastics aside, I did not think I could conform to this new way of thinking, of believing. It was just asking too much.

There had been a slight glimmer of hope near the end of the class. He mentioned something called the *Law of Graduality.* It refers to the idea that if you run into a very difficult teaching, you can take all the time you need to digest the truth, trusting that God will show you the way, BUT... you have to leave room for that to happen. Was I willing to consider that what he said about Mary could possibly be true? I think he saw me drifting-off, possibly deciding to reject his "Mary," which would have meant leaving behind that which had captivated my spiritual senses with its heavenly aroma and made me hungrily long for nothing else. I was so close. It was all going so well, up until today. Today, the Terrible! Today the END! Today...her. Yes, today HER! And today her: wonderful, beautiful, kind, gentle, loving, humble, sweet and just what I needed...her.

But I get ahead of myself. Where to start? My birth? My re-birth? My thousand little deaths? I'm so boring and so small and He and what He does is so much more interesting, but to give you a frame of reference of who He was dealing with, this may be helpful. I will try to be brief.

Let's start at the beginning. I was born in Houston, Texas, the granddaughter of a Southern Baptist minister and daughter of a Texas oil man and a world-class Bible teaching mom. I was the youngest of three daughters, and we were raised "Texas Proud." Some of my earliest memories are riding in the back of a flat bed pick up that we called the "hick-up truck" with my sisters, racing down a dusty, hot, dirt road squealing with delight, bandana head scarves flapping in the breeze. We were taught to love God, His Word, country, family, and all things "'merican!" We were also taught to share this love and to be kindhearted to everyone we met. My grandmother was a shining example. Thanksgiving at her house was like a mini United Nations assembly session. We would be eating Lebanese meat pies and Vietnamese dumplings, brought by several of her "families," while the Mariachi band my sister befriended at a local Mexican restaurant would play "La Bamba" between bites of turkey. This is how we loved and served God, by evangelizing (telling and sharing the Good News of Jesus) especially to those who were not Christians.

"Not Christian" was a vast array of people. Catholics were definitely in that category. I was not taught what they were exactly, but they were not Christians (or at least not our kind of Christians), and therefore, we were to be wary. We were to love them, for sure, but to look on them as people who needed "straightening out." Most importantly, they needed to be taught the Bible, as it was unfathomable and against all we believed that one could be a Christian and not know or at least want to know the Bible cover to cover.

As a Baptist, that is how we experienced Jesus—not through sacrament, but through His Word. And, just to be clear about what a Southern Baptist is, I'll shed a little light on my particular upbringing. We were far more than a list of do's and don'ts. We were people who really, deeply loved God. Yet we were often mistakenly called "snake handlers" or "pew jumpers" by the uninformed. We were certainly not that. Baptists share a history with the very reserved Puritans, not the far more exciting Pentecostals. We were told "no drinking, dancing, smoking, nor gambling" (which included dice, cards, and betting on BINGO...but oddly enough, not dominoes for some strange reason). These were all prohibited. We did not believe that the gifts of the Holy Spirit were still active (no "funny business" as I was told). There could be no revelation after the Bible had been written—no "divine healings," no "speaking in tongues," no "supernatural manifestations" of any kind, really. Just the BIBLE—Sola- Scriptura—"The Bible Alone." Later in life, I did wonder what happened to all of those beautiful gifts listed in 1 Corinthians, Chapter 12. I had read the Bible many times over and, quite frankly, had never found an expiration date on them. But as you can see, the stories of the saints, the Eucharistic feast, divine grace imparted through the sacraments, and so many other of the Church's teachings were for us imaginary fairy tales or witchcraft, or hocus-pocus, from which we were to keep a safe distance.

I distinctly remember my mother telling me that the only Democrat my very staunch Democratic Baptist grandfather had refused to vote for was John F. Kennedy, because he was a Catholic. And what I heard from my grandfather, or read from his collection of books stated that the Pope was not only unchristian...but that he was possibly the "devil himself." Therefore, I assumed that all things coming from him or from the Catholic Church were not from God. The signs I read advertising Parish Bingo Night were evidence enough of that! Who was I to argue with my grandfather? He was the one who knew the Bible so well and had inspired my mother and me to become Bible teachers. I believed him when he said that what was not strictly in the Bible would lead to false doctrine and apostasy. So, quite obviously, I was more than a little dubious of Catholic Church teaching, traditions, the sacraments, and the saints. "Aren't we all saints?" I reasoned. And the most astonishing thing I learned about Catholics was that they worshiped idols! I was erroneously taught that Catholics worshipped Mary, prayed to statues and, worst of all, did something called "Eucharistic Adoration," which of course, we absolutely did not understand... staring at *Bread?* I was told that these faulty practices were "false gods and detestable to the Lord" and could possibly land me in hell if I had *anything* to do with them. I was to avoid them at all cost or else run the risk of offending my God, Whom I loved so much. So, as I grew up, the very thought of being a Catholic was actually not only very strange and confusing to me. It was terrifying!

"Hate what is evil and cling to what is good." This is what we learned as Baptists. It was not out of a heart of malice that our suspicion of Catholicism was born, but out of a heart trying to please God in all that we did. My thinking was very much like St. Pauls' before his conversion experience. St. Paul, a learned Pharisee who persecuted and killed early Christians, also truly thought what he was doing was right, and he too had elders to back him up.

Fast-forward a handful of years and many thousands of miles traveled from Texas. I married the most handsome and devout man who happened to be my dear friend from high school, and we moved to Washington, DC. He became a highly respected architect and I worked in the design field. In time, we were blessed with four wonderful daughters. After the birth of our first child, I left my design work to start an interdenominational women's Bible study program. By God's grace, several years after the birth of our third child my husband and I had inched our way slowly, slowly, sacramentally into the Anglican Church, for reasons you will read about later. There I considered myself to be the "Protestant Poster Child," the world's happiest Protestant. Though my life was not perfect, I felt I had at last found a home in the church where we belonged. It had a wonderful mix of sound Bible teaching, worship, healing prayer, and a great youth program for our kids. All was going so well, what more could I want?

Then it came.

The challenge.

No, the wake up call.

With a flash of a blinding smile punctuated by hot pink lipstick, five-foot-two, tanned and brilliantly bedazzled Janice, one of the wonderful women whom I had the privilege of teaching for about twenty years in the Bible study, had the nerve to come up to me and say, "I have finally found someone who loves Jesus more than you do!"

Smirk!

I was so caught off guard.

"WHAT!? No way!" I said, brushing her comment aside.

"Oh, yes I have," she persisted, "and…he is a Catholic priest!"

Now I *knew* she wasn't telling the truth!

"Everyone knows that Catholic priests don't love Jesus! They only love Mary!" I exclaimed. And then my internal dialogue starting to kick in. "Silly Janice!" I thought dismissively.

But she insisted. "Oh he really does! You just have to meet him! And, by the way, he works at a retreat center, so if you go and meet him, maybe you could see if we can use his center for our Bible study retreat."

"Hmmm," I thought. "Well, we do need a venue for the spring retreat, and I would *really* like to meet someone she thinks loves Jesus more than I do—just so I can prove her *wrong*! She just must not know what she is talking about. Catholic priest! Ha!"

"Okay," I said. "You're on!"

After getting his number from her, I called him and made an appointment. I wanted to check this off my to-do list and lovingly put her in her place. I can't really remember what I was thinking when I drove to the retreat center. I had, over the years, met many amazing Catholics and therefore softened on my stance, thinking now that perhaps not *all* Catholics were going to hell, though I was still very confused about what exactly they *did* believe. Even with this new insight I was a bit nervous about having our retreat at a Catholic center. I had, out of necessity (so I thought), sent my girls to Catholic schools in the District of Columbia. They offered a very good education at a very fair price. But we had not engaged in the parish. I was very quick to teach my kids all that we did not believe nor have in common with Catholics, (but never pointed out all that we did have in common.)

And so, I parked my car and unsuspectingly made my way in to meet the man whom God would use to change my life forever.

One of the many great things about God is His sense of humor. He is always full of surprises, as Pope

Francis would say. Of course, at the time, I did not find any of this a bit funny.

First of all, the retreat center was beautiful, warm, light-filled, and welcoming. For some reason, I had expected it to be cold, dark, and institutional, mirroring what I thought the Church was like. And I was equally surprised when I met the priests who were not at all what I was expecting. They were a group of very young, warm, funny, joyful, kind, handsome, and sincere men. For some reason, I had thought they would be stiff-necked and old, personified dogmas (though I had never read a dogma and did not exactly know what one was), instead of real live flesh and blood filled with God's holy fire.

And then, I met him—Fr. Michael. The minute I spoke to him, I knew I had been bested. Janice was right! He did love Jesus more than I did! He did! He knew Jesus like I did not. I could see it. It was in his eyes, in his voice, in his words, in his mannerisms. It was Jesus! Everywhere! He was focused and mission driven. He was like an arctic tanker cutting his way through deep ice. There was no stopping him. I knew that he had something I did not. But what? How? I had the sweetest, most intimate relationship with the Lord. He was my best friend. He was my all, my everything. I had read the Bible daily since I was twelve and I thought I knew Him like no other. But still, he, this *priest* had something more! How? I needed to know. I wanted what he had. The light switch was turned on to me seeing that perhaps there was still a

great deal more to learn about my faith, but I did not
dare ask, so I listened.

To this day, I have no idea what he thought of me
back then. I knew he knew of me and the women I
taught, as he saw quite a few of them on a regular basis
for a sort of spiritual coaching. I do not know if he
knew from the start what God was about to do in my
life. All I know is that near the end of our
conversation, after he had given me a tour of the
retreat center and tried to explain to me the statue of
the Sacred Heart of Jesus (I might as well have had
feathers in my ears), and after…after…after what
seemed like forever, I could take it no more.

I blurted out, "What is it!? What do you have that I
don't have? Janice told me that you love Jesus more
than I do, and I believe she may be right!"
He smiled and, with a bit of a chuckle, and a humble
shrug of his shoulders, simply said, "It's the
Eucharist."

I sat down, a bit stunned, but feeling that what he said
was true. All I could say was, "*I knew it!*" And how *did*
I know? It had been revealed to me years before, but
at that time, I was not ready to take it all in.

He then encouraged me, "Try going to an Adoration
Chapel. You'll see," he said.

"Anything but that!" I thought. "Why would he tell me
to go there?" Instead, I reasoned that if I just talked to

him a while longer, I could figure it all out without having to go that far out of my comfort zone.

We decided to pray about whether he would be willing to see me regularly about spiritual matters. He then invited me to join a small weekly Catechism class that he would lead. He invited Janice and another Catholic friend who was exploring her faith more deeply to join us as well. I told him that there was really no need for me to take the class as I would *never* become a Catholic, but he argued that, if half of the women I taught in the Bible study were Catholic, shouldn't I know at least what they believed? He sounded so…reasonable.

I prayed about it and felt the Lord's urging, and so we began to meet weekly for the class and, much to my surprise, I was agreeing with most of what Fr. Michael was saying. I began to read the Catechism and found it beautiful, a real treasure. I had thought it would be as inspiring as reading the phone book, but much to my delight it was a true gift from the Church. It was the collection of about two thousand years of wisdom and commentary on the Book I loved the most, the Bible. I could not believe I had been a Christian for so long and had missed out entirely on reading this treasure. I was beginning to feel, against all odds, that despite everything I was taught to fear, avoid, and disbelieve, the Lord might possibly be calling me to become, of all things, a Catholic! How could it be?

This period of discernment was tumultuous and confounding. Until I *knew* what I was to do, I told no one but my husband and Fr. Michael what was taking place in my soul. I was in great anguish keeping this "secret," but since I was still just exploring possibilities, I did not want to upset anyone close to me until the Lord made very clear the path that I was to take.

Fr. Michael continued to urge me to go to the Adoration Chapel, but I was too afraid of possibly offending my God. I knew that there was something "Other" in there, something I did not understand, because God, in His loving and very kind way had given me a glimpse of Himself, heaven on earth, a few years earlier. I was hungry now and I was seeking Him like never before and I felt, if I asked, He would answer me. Little did I know He was going to give me a great deal more than I could ever have dared to hope for. All that stood in the way was a three-number pass code, a great deal of fear, and forty-five years of hard-wired Protestant theology.

But...before I unlocked the door to the Adoration Chapel, a door in my heart had to be pried open. The state of my hardened heart reminded me of the Pre-Raphaelite painting entitled "The Light of the World" in which William Holman Hunt depicts Christ standing on the outside of a dwelling in the dark, holding an illuminated lantern and knocking at a door, ancient and overgrown with weeds. Curiously, there is no handle on the exterior. The door can be opened only from the inside, and that is right where I found myself. It was not the lock on the outside of the Adoration Chapel door that kept me away, but the bar on the inside of my heart. Had there not been an encouraging rapping a few years earlier by our loving Lord, I would never had had the courage to press the buttons to unlock the door and experience that which would lead me much, much closer to Him.

**Praise:** Thank you Lord for the *Law of Graduality*, a gift from the Church, a chance to explore the Faith more fully, go deeper and open to all.

**Prayer:** Lord, please give me an open mind and a teachable heart to seek You beyond my own understanding or fears. Always give me the grace of allowing the *Law of Graduality* to work in my life so that I do not fall into religious ossification and become inflexible, unable to be bent and molded into new shapes that more resemble You.

**Promise**: Paul speaking, "May the eyes of your heart be illuminated, so that you may know what is the hope of his calling, and the wealth of the glory of his inheritance with the saints…" Ephesians 1:18

**Proof of the Promise**: I have learned that if we will allow room for the Holy Spirit to shed light on our heart even the slightest bit, God will reveal Himself and His Truth to us. He will more than exceed our greatest expectations.

**Ponder: Journal here** about your own upbringing. What is *your* story? Are there parts of your faith that as an adult you might want to inquire about further? If so…what are they?

Perhaps take these issues to your priest, pastor or spiritual director.

## Chapter 2

*"There is not a single moment when God is not communicating himself to us. Most of what occurs in our lives seems to happen accidentally and at random. Now and then God reveals his presence. At times we see the thread and we thank him, but he is always there; everything speaks of him." --Wilfrid Stinissen,* Into Your Hands, Father- Abandoning Ourselves to the God Who Loves Us," *pg 23.*

*The Lord is always calling us to a new encounter, but at times it can be so hard to hear Him. Often I am deafened by internal*

*struggles, like my preconceived notions or my childhood training,*
 *and sometimes life itself just throws me for a loop, and I can't*
 *think of anything else but the situation at hand and the trials*
 *that it brings. But then, He comes... the Word speaks to my*
 *hurting, perplexed heart, and because of or in spite of the stress,*
 *anxiety or pain, I listen...*

## Seeking

In late 2001, the world was recovering from the aftermath of 9-11, and a group of my friends were, in their own way, waging a personal war on terrorism of the most intimate kind. The name of this terrorist was very familiar and continues to destroy many thousands of lives yearly. Cancer. The enemy. It hit my three friends hard, and its initial onslaught left shaken children wondering if their mothers would recover, and husbands weary to the bone. I felt the Lord calling me to help them in some way. He seemed to want to reach out to them through me. I felt totally ill prepared to help.

I had come a long way in my beliefs about prayer. I knew that God still worked in miraculous ways through it, even today. About that time, I was introduced to the Order of Saint Luke, a healing prayer ministry. This set my friends and me on a mission--to pray and look for "gifted healers" with the hope of finding a cure for them. By God's grace, we encountered many beautifully anointed souls. I saw first-hand that something good always happens when we pray. My friends' lives were miraculously sustained for a short while. Peace would wash over us like transparent, supernatural waves that buoyed and transported our souls, renewing, refreshing, and sustaining us. But sadly, ultimately, as will be the case for every life, my three friends passed on to the next realm, each carried off by a final wave of peace, like a boat setting sail for another shore. All three were Catholic.

My friend Joannie was numbered among those ladies and she was one of the holiest souls I had ever known. She was so sure of her faith. She was also equally confident about the power of the sacraments to draw us to God. As we would travel from one healing prayer center to the next, she would lie on her bed at night and read to me. She would say, "Melissa, you know that the Eucharist really *is* the Body and Blood of Christ, or He would never have said so!" I could not argue. She knew I believed the Bible—cover-to-cover, and she drew my attention to John 6:48-66, a passage about the Eucharist. She argued that Jesus was not speaking figuratively when He called Himself the Bread of Life and urged us to eat His Body. Many of His disciples left Him, she reminded me, because "This is a difficult statement, Who can listen to it?"

I had to decide. Was Jesus speaking the truth, and was I going to believe Him…or not? She was so emphatic. Again and again she would read it to me. "Listen," she would say, "Listen again!" and away she would go reading it to me. Finally I said, "Yes, Joannie! I do believe that the Eucharist is the Body and Blood, Soul and Divinity of Christ, but maybe not quite like you do!" I honestly was not exactly sure what I believed, but I did know this: in the healing ministry, the

Eucharist is held in very high esteem. I could not deny what I had seen at these services and Masses, and I knew that there was much more to the Eucharist than I could explain.

On June 14, 2003, I received terrible news as I was on my way to a beloved retreat center in Leakey, Texas, to drop off my daughters at a Christian camp. My girls and I had stopped for lunch in a very tiny bend in the road called Comfort, and it was there, in such a sweetly named rock-hewn Texas town, that I heard that Joannie had passed away. What came to my head was the verse, "Praise be to the God and Father of our Lord Jesus Christ, the Father of Compassion and the God of all comfort, who comforts us in all our troubles...For just as we share abundantly in the sufferings of Christ, so also our comfort abounds through Christ." Words I so desperately needed to hear right then. I managed to get back to DC for the funeral and return to the retreat center, but I was so distraught by her death that I had trouble functioning. I could not believe that she was gone. She was so holy that I honestly wondered if she would come back from the dead at her funeral. It was that hard to accept her death. She was so passionate, so on fire. How could it be? How could she be gone?

Joanie's words, "It really is Him!" kept haunting me. Could what she had said about the Eucharist actually be true? I had too many questions swirling around in my head while the deep, deep sorrow of losing a beloved friend ached in my bones. Graciously, for the next two weeks, the Lord allowed me to be placed at the retreat center deep in the heart of the canyon. Like Moses, I felt safely tucked away, hidden in the cleft of the Rock. (Exodus 33:22) I was swaddled by prayerful people who were so lovingly supporting me. But, in spite of genuine concern and a profuse abundance of wisdom, no one was able to give me the answer to the question Joanie left behind.

Finally, in absolute desperation, I decided to take my trouble, my questions, my doubts, and my fears directly to God. I decided to put Him to the test as I never had before. I resolved to see if He would answer me, as He had so many others in the Bible, if I asked with a very sincere and earnest heart. At the risk of being presumptuous, I reasoned, "If *they* had heard from God, why not me, too?"

My courage came from the fact that I had read the Bible many times, and that one of the things I so loved about it was the very humanness of its characters. All are flawed people with real problems, real stories, and real lives. If God would stoop so low as to speak to them, would He, in fact, humble Himself to speak to me? I would never know unless I asked. And so I did.

I packed a water bottle and I hit the trail. Up, up, up the canyon I went, higher and higher with each step. The cedar tree droppings and the chalky limestone rocks covered the path and low scrubby bushes led the way. Finally, I came to a nice clearing where I could see over the canyon edge down to the river below. I sat on a large, rough, lichen-covered rock. Once I settled in, I very boldly and resolutely told God that I would not move until He answered me, once and for all, about the Eucharist.

What a state I was in as I sat there! I hadn't been able to sleep, and felt as if God had been keeping me awake at night to ponder all that Joannie had told me. I was exhausted from grief and I knew that when I returned home, I would have to face my other two heroic but dying friends—one already in hospice. I was near my breaking point. I felt that I needed to stop "wasting valuable energy" on a question only God could answer. I had read and read until I could read no more about the Eucharist and sacraments. The Christian Churches, represented by brilliant and well-meaning men and women, could not agree on what the Eucharist is exactly or how it comes into being. There were as many answers as there were denominations. What to do? Who to believe? So there I waited, perched upon my rock, for The Ancient of Days to speak to me, a mere nothing, lowly and miserable, desperately seeking the answer to what I believed to be life's greatest question.

In the most reverential way, I stated my purpose. "Dear Lord, here I sit. You know that I try to love You with all of my heart as best I can. And You have all knowledge and understanding, and so it comes as no surprise to You that I long to be enlightened, as strange as it sounds, as to whether You really do come to earth, as my dear friend said, in the form of a *cracker*. And, if You do, You are aware that I do not want to miss one single crumb of You while I am alive on this planet. But if this is wrong, please, I beg You, please,

please let me know now and set me free from this obsession."

I waited. Nothing. I waited and waited. Still nothing. It seemed like days, but I know it was only hours. I began to doubt everything, most of all myself, for being so stupid for putting God to this foolish test. But I had nothing to lose at this point, and nothing left to give to this endeavor but my patient suffering. I longed for Him to answer me.

Eventually, my intellectual curiosity was spent; my emotional well, wept dry; my physical energy exhausted; my spiritual interior, at a point of utter and complete bankruptcy. I was at the rock-bottom seabed of my soul and I needed an answer in order to have the will to push back to the surface for air. I pleaded again, "Lord, I am most sincere. You are aware that I am absolutely distraught and do not want to go on living if I am missing any part of You in any way! If I am to experience You like this, please, please reveal Yourself to me and answer." And then, honestly, much to my great astonishment, He did.

"Get up." I heard. I was not sure if this voice was audible or in my inner spirit. I obeyed, scrambling off of my rock, hurriedly uncrossing my legs, which had fallen asleep, and were now speckled with small purplish dots where tiny sharp pebbles had left their imprint on my ankle bones. Blood rushed back into my limbs making them tingle and buzz all the more.

"Now, look over the canyon's edge." At this point, I was wondering if He would ask me to jump! Much to my great relief He simply said, "Look and see how beautiful it is."

"Yes, Lord, it is beautiful."

"No! Really look at how beautiful this is. Look at the water, the trees, the sky, and the birds."

"Yes, Lord, I see."

"No! Really look! Look at the canyon and the clouds and rocks and the colors. Look and see all I have created."

"Yes, Lord, I see. It is beyond anything man could do."

And what came next made me know that this was not an imaginary conversation. What He was about to say was nothing I could have ever thought of by myself. It was such a surprise!

"What you see that is so beautiful, is all fallen!" Then He asked me a question. "Do you think anything or anyone in this fallen world could receive Me except by my grace?"

"No, Lord, I do not."

"Well then, no man can give to you what only I can give to you, and no man can keep from you what only I can give you."

"Okay, Lord. If that is true, please give to me Yourself now." And He did.

It was a most beautiful experience of Love and Light. I was completely enveloped in peace, and His presence flooded my heart, mind, and soul as never before. I am not sure how long it lasted, but in this experience I was given a beautiful picture. It was a three-paneled altarpiece, a triptych. In the center panel was a chalice, the Eucharistic cup being held up by priestly hands, and above it was the Host, broken and blessed, as when the priest holds it up during the Mass and says, "Behold the Lamb of God, behold Him Who takes away the sins of the world. Blessed are those called to the supper of the Lamb." Only it was not a picture—it was more like a window—and I was witnessing it eternally live. I felt like all time, history, present and future collapsed into this one moment.

On the panel to the right was the Crucifixion. It was Christ, not a picture of Christ, but Christ, on the cross, broken and bleeding in agonizing pain, for me. He said nothing. He only looked at me—no, more like *in* me. I will never forget His look of love. I could not breath. My Savior, there, for me? To say that I felt unworthy of the sacrifice is beyond telling. No human language has strong enough words to express this. It was as if there had been a huge mistake. I knew that it was me that was supposed to be there-- not Him...yet there He hung. It left me sick with love, humbled and eternally thankful.

The third panel to the left was even more curious, as it was a window into the Church. It was as if I were standing at the altar looking into the congregation, into pew after pew of familiar faces—all in row after row, nothing but a sea of people, all staring forward at me, some blinking, some smiling, dressed in their Sunday best--ready to hear me speak, only no words came out. Then above the triptych, these words came blazing and on fire, like gold coming out of a crucible, molten hot then cooling to brightest gold: "This is My Body, broken for you." And below, "Do this in remembrance of Me."

I awoke. There I lay in a soft nest of cedar needles. I had absolute peace. I will tell you, I had no idea what had happened. All I knew was that, for the first time in a long time, the agonizing gnawing at my soul was quieted. I did not know the answer still. It would take years to process all that I had just experienced. But I knew Who had the answers and I knew that there was a great deal more I would need to discover and experience about the God of grace Who had so graciously answered me.

**Praise:** Thank You Lord that You showed me, "This is My Body broken for you..."

**Prayer:** Lord, please open my heart and reveal Yourself to me, speak to me so that I can know Who You are, that You are near and that You love me, even in my miserable state. Reveal Yourself to me in any of a thousand different ways in which You speak daily to all. Let me experience You specifically, in the Eucharist, through Your Son in prayer, in Your Sacred Word, and through Your Body, the Church.

**Promise:** "You shall seek me. And you will find me, when you have sought me with your whole heart," Jeremiah 29:13

**Proof of the Promise:** Ultimately, only God can reveal Himself to us. I have learned that the Lord shows Himself to those who pray for the grace of an open heart and a sincere spirit. If we have a desire to know Him, it is because He Himself has put it there in the first place. He will be found, if we keep seeking.

**Ponder: Journal here** a conversation you would like to have with God asking Him for the grace to be a seeker: to want to know and trust Him more. Ask Him for the grace to make you hungry for the things of Him, giving you an open heart to receive Him in new ways. If you have fears or hesitations about knowing Him more deeply -- if you're not there yet-- ask Him for a desire to want to be there...it is all by His grace.

## Chapter 3

*"I am the bread of life. Whoever comes to me will never go hungry, and whoever believes in me will never be thirsty." John 6:35*

*In spite of all of my fears, the Lord was gently invited me into a great unknown that I had been cautioned against my entire life, even though the teaching was as old as the Church itself. In order to be transformed to more resemble Him, I had to trust that He knew what He was doing even if I did not. There, He enabled me to leave myself behind so He could embrace me all the more...*

## Doors Unlocked

So there I stood, outside of the Adoration Chapel door. I had come a long way since my profound encounter with God in the canyon. Watching others hold the Eucharist in such high esteem and realizing I could experience Him in a physical way, differently than I could in prayer or through His sacred Word or through other people, had made me long to be in a congregation of like-minded worshipers who were more "sacramental" than we were in the Presbyterian church.

By now I had been a Baptist, availing myself not of sacraments, but of ordinances, which are seen as symbols performed out of obedience to the Lord's command to "remember Him." Next, we had become Bible Church goers (very similar to Baptists in their strong Biblical beliefs, but with a more contemporary "praise and worship" atmosphere), and then Presbyterians. As Presbyterians, we were more formal in our liturgy, but did not believe that the Host is the True Body and Blood of Jesus. And now, here I stood, a very happy and contented Anglican, who was quite sacramental, standing outside of an Adoration Chapel at a Catholic Church! God had been wooing me all along and I had, by His grace, inched my way ever closer theologically to Catholicism. But was I able to jump over that last hurdle to embrace what I believed to be true? Could I concede that perhaps there was still a great deal more to learn about God's desire to unite with me--and that His plan included the Eucharist? To accept this, I would have to admit that the theology I lived by, and had for many years taught others to believe as well, was incomplete. If I had been missing something, would I have the courage to rethink it all? Could I do that?

I stood on a precipice and I knew it. God had not asked me to jump from the canyon wall in Texas, but He was now asking me to take a leap of faith and to trust Him to catch me.

But would I? Had the lock in my heart been tumbled enough to allow passage?

I had dashed past the chapel so many times before with one eye closed, as I did not want my "eyes to cause me to sin" (Matthew 5:29) by looking at something I deemed to be offensive to God. In spite of what God had shown me in the canyon those years before, old habits die hard, and my brain and spirit could not keep from remembering what it had known since childhood. Somewhere deep inside of me I kept hearing "Beware!" The Adoration Chapel represented idol worship to me and I wanted NO PART of idolatry! So day after day, as I took my little ones to school, grabbing their tiny, trusting hands, we would pass by—no, rush past at breakneck speed—to get beyond the Adoration Chapel as fast as possible.

Still, I was deeply curious. I wondered, for example, why they kept whatever was behind that door under a code lock, since the other doors to the Church were always open. I had concluded that the Catholics kept some sort of deep magic in there, shrouded with secrecy and guarded with care. Some days, I imagined

all kinds of evils taking place behind that door. And I was very perplexed that I never saw anyone go into the chapel. Very curious, indeed. If the content of the chapel was so precious that it needed to be protected by key code, why was not everyone flocking to it? What on earth was going on in there? Obviously nothing "earthly," but I had absolutely no idea, and had decided to stay as far away as possible…
Until today.

There I stood! My mind was a battlefield. My heart longed to go in. If the true Body and Blood, Soul and Divinity of Jesus Christ Himself was behind the door, how could I stay outside? My Lord? My God, in there? And I, outside on the sidewalk? With all of these other passers by… just idly having everyday conversations about groceries and hair appointments, meetings and dog walkers? With Jesus Christ waiting, just behind this door?

I was an anxious, conflicted mess… a tumultuous ball of contradictory reasoning. "Double minded" best summed me up. James 1:6 states, "for the one who doubts is like a wave of the sea that is driven and tossed about by the wind." Needless to say, I had no peace.

One half of my mind was howling at me, "Don't go in! How could you? Why are you doing this? Who knows what you will find behind this door? What if they do sacrifices in there? What if you are possessed by an evil spirit when you enter? What if you are seen by one of your Bible study members and this makes her start asking questions you are not ready to answer? You might lead her astray and you know the punishment for that... 'It would be better for him if a millstone were put around his neck and he be thrown into the sea than for him to cause one of these little ones to sin.'[Luke 17:2]] And your own little ones! What about them? What would your *mother* think? Worse, what about your grandfather? And your grandmother? And all of your family? What about your husband? He is a vestry member! How could you betray them all? How could you allow one priest to influence you to this degree? Have you lost your mind? You should RUN! No, you should withdraw your children from Catholic school and forget this ever happened! Now! Run and never walk this way again, then everything will be fine and you will be safe and back to 'normal.'"

My wiser self knew I could not run. Running away because of fear was not an option today. As I stood there shaking, wondering what to do, my sane, still, quiet, reasonable interior voice started to whisper, "Now wait a minute. It's just a room for prayer! What could be so bad about that? And almost half of the women that go to your Bible study are Catholic! So how could it be so evil? You loved Joannie and now Fr. Michael, Fr. Dave, Monsignor Duffy, Francis MacNutt, and Mother Teresa, and your friends, Linda and Margy and Gino. Are any of them 'possessed' or crazy? And didn't you see for yourself that Fr. Michael, who has been encouraging you to go to Adoration, is on fire for God and completely dedicated to Jesus Christ? He would not lead you astray. If this is what God has in store for you, He will provide a way for your husband and children and all those who know you to understand that you are only doing what He is calling you to do—to walk in obedience, even if you don't understand it all yourself. And hasn't this been a good school for all of your children? Do not worry, have faith, and remember what you saw in the canyon. It is all by His grace. Trust in Him."

The word, "Help!" erupted from my soul, the prayer of a desperate person—the one that God so loves to answer. As I uttered that word, the Lord in His most gracious manner sent an "angel" to my aid. (As the word "angel" means "messenger," I feel I have many sent to me daily to deliver just the word I need to hear in the moment.) Jen was a beautiful new friend who, through God's loving providence, was not only a member of my Bible study; she was someone I trusted. She was also a relatively recent convert to Catholicism. She "just happened" to walk up to me in the middle of my manic deliberations.

With her kind words she first provided the access code to the door. All of the Church members had it. But she did more than grant access to the physical door. She was able to bolster my spirit with the words of reassurance that I needed to hear to help unlock my interior door. Jen assured me that there was nothing horrible inside! There was only a beautiful golden box with small rounded doors that I would need to open in order to view the Blessed Host. She was late for a meeting at work so she had to walk on, but her loving and kind words gave me the confidence I needed to be able to utter the next prayer outside that door.

"Here I am Lord, Your girl. And I am seeking You once again, hopefully with a pure heart and pure intentions. You know that I want to know You more and love You better. If what I am about to do will offend You in ANY WAY, I want to apologize before I do it, and I ask that You will forgive me because I am going in trusting what I believe to be signs from You and people You have placed upon my path to guide me. If You could be so gracious as to allow me to know that if this is REALLY YOU in there, that You would please make it perfectly clear, right away, as I would like to not miss You a single day in this way for the rest of my life. And if it's not true, so be it."

With that, I took a very deep breath and pressed the numbers that would change my heart, my mind, and the course of my journey to eternity.

I was in. It was dark. Only a candle flickered on the altar next to the tabernacle. Much to my amazement, it was so peaceful. It felt so holy, not scary at all. The walls were beige and there was a crimson red velvet curtain hanging on the wall behind the tabernacle that set it off as the focal point of the room. I bent down and looked at the beautiful dark, square, wooden box. It reminded me of my Old Testament studies where I learned that the Jewish temple in Jerusalem contained the presence of God in the place called the Holy of Holies—a cube, made of wood overlaid with gold. This Holy of Holies had an ornate, highly polished golden square front façade, and in the center of it was a pair of circular golden doors, cut right down the middle, with small handles to open and see what was inside. These little doors, in a funny way, brought back memories of sugar Easter eggs I used to have as a child. I would peek into them and wonder at the surprise inside which symbolized new life in Christ, rebirth and resurrection joy. The little doors of the tabernacle were surrounded by an elaborately embossed golden "necklace" with four inlaid crimson rubies that could be seen even when the doors were opened, to remind us that it is by His wounds on the cross that we have access to Him now. Around the necklace were eight "rays" of silver, each containing a sculpted sheath of wheat. And in between those, lay sixteen smaller silver rays, two between each larger ray of wheat, resembling sharp, piercing nails. It was very beautiful.

I felt a bit awkward opening the little doors. I was not sure if someone who actually knew what they were doing might walk in and catch me doing something wrong. But here I was and I was going to finish what I had started. I once again said a prayer and opened the two little doors. There He was. Refined and Holy. There was a cross etched on the Blessed Host and I noticed that it was not directly straight up and down and I wondered why. Then I thought, "Well, if man has anything to do with this…it will never be 'perfectly displayed'… 'all by His grace.'" There I stood with a thousand questions, doubts and fears racing through my mind. Four kneelers were placed in front of the tabernacle so I decided to kneel down using one toward the side. There was a cross cut out of the kneeler in front of me and so I sat back and decided to look through the cut-out of the cross to see if I could

view the tabernacle, and I could. I realized then that it is only when looking through the lens of the cross that we can see clearly all that God has done for us.
I then prayed the boldest prayer I had ever prayed, and that says a great deal, considering what I had asked up until now. I said, "Okay, here I am. You got me here. If You are really here, please show me now. It's now or never, God.  Please let me know if you are really physically here."  I waited.

Nothing. I waited a bit longer… and then He acted.

A floodgate of His love burst open, pouring out from the tabernacle, overwhelming me like nothing I had ever experienced. Peace, Light, Joy, and LOVE! I was flooded by Love. I was floating in Love and on Love and under Love and breathing Love and Love was in me and I was in LOVE! It was fantastic! It was so joyful! It was so freeing! It was physical and spiritual and mental and emotional.  I was swimming in Him and He in me. It was an ocean of Light and it was spectacular! It quieted all of my fears and doubts and questions, as "Perfect Love casts out all fear."[1 John 4:18] It was *HIM*! There was no doubt it was Jesus.
 The experience of Love lasted for quite some time and it was all I needed to know. It was "Complete." It was "Shalom" in the truest sense of the word, absolute Wholeness. All I could do was say, "I am so sorry, Lord! I have judged rashly about things I did not understand. Please forgive me and thank You for revealing Yourself to me in this way, now."

I heard a voice in my inner spirit and it said, "Don't be so quick to judge, Missy!" (Missy is what my dad called me when I was a child.) But there was no condemnation in the voice. It was a voice of love, and it even sounded as if He were smiling, because I had been made aware of my shortcomings even before He spoke.

All I could do was weep. I wept and wept and wept. I wept out of sorrow and out of joy. I wept and wept and wept some more. I had been dismissive and even ridiculed others' beliefs about things that were sacred to them—things about which I had no idea. I had lacked a "teachable spirit" and instead was almost arrogant in my beliefs. I wept bitter tears of remorse for having been so puffed up and prideful. And then I wept for joy! I felt the Lord's loving hand comfort me. I was overwhelmed by all I had just realized about HIM and me. Something in the deepest part of me was touched, released and transformed. An inner healing was taking place that I did not even know I needed. I was healed and there was peace, perfect peace.

It would take a long while to sort it all out, but I did know this—I had some apologies to make and I needed to start immediately! As soon as I got home, I began to call those whose beliefs I had dismissed to tell them how sorry I was. My friends were befuddled but listened attentively, saying… "I don't really know what you are talking about, but okay, you are forgiven! No worries!" It felt so good! I was beginning to feel freer and freer with each apology. God was liberating me from myself, little by little. There was progress—I felt it, yes, but I still had a long way to go. Our Lord was by no means finished with me yet.

**Praise:** Lord, You are gentle and all knowing. You long for me to know You as You really are and You prepared my heart to receive the truth of You years before I was able to understand and accept it. I praise You God, for revealing to me that You are in the Eucharist.

**Prayer:** Thank you for revealing Yourself so plainly to me in the Eucharist. When I have doubts, or feel judgemental or unloving, please replace these thoughts with faith in You and Your Word. Let me not rely on my emotions or even my own faulty reasoning, but on You and Your Word and Truth.

**Promise:** "Therefore, if you, though you are evil, know how to give good gifts to your sons, how much more will your Father, who is in heaven give good things to those who ask him?" Matthew 7:11

**Proof of the Promise:** I have learned that we should not be dismissive and judgmental of other's sacred beliefs. We are to respect what others deem to be holy. We should pray for an open and teachable spirit and courage to trust in Him because He will never give His children snakes when we ask for Bread.

**Ponder: Journal here** about *your* personal understanding of the Eucharist? After you're finished, see appendix 1 for some inspiration.

## Chapter 4

*I sought the LORD, and he answered me, delivered me from all my fears.* Psalm 34:5

*Questions, fears, doubts, they are all a part of the journey. God in His loving and patient way, reveals truth to us as we are able to accept it. He began to set me free little by little and it felt so wonderful, I kept longing for more...*

### The Way

Day after day I would return to the Adoration Chapel. I confess it was addicting. The room was so peaceful and womb-like. The overpowering experience of the first day never repeated itself; I simply went and sat and prayed. Since I had been a baptized Christian from the age of eight, born into a Christian family, I had been taught to have a daily time of prayer from an early age. This time had now become my "quiet time" before the Lord.

In the Adoration chapel, I would simply read and pray and enjoy His presence, and soon would learn He enjoyed mine too! This was a new thought for me, that *I* could actually delight *Him*. I felt I had worked hard to be a "good person" all of my life (well, just about all of my life), and for some reason had always felt like "gold plated poop," but was never really sure why.

Catholicism, the sacraments, and the mystery of it all were becoming very appealing to me. Jesus had totally engaged my heart. (A friend questioned if I was having an affair.) I was totally in love with Jesus in an entirely new way. But as a Bible teacher, I was feeling that my head needed to catch up to my heart. This prompted me to stay up for hours and hours late at night reading Scott Hahn, Francis Beckwith, Blessed John Henry Newman, St. Thomas Aquinas, St. Augustine, and a myriad of other Catholic writers, many of whom were converts themselves. My biblical education up to this point had included the Bible and anything written post-reformation. I had now discovered fifteen hundred years of collective genius from which to learn. I was like a kid in a candy store, delighted beyond all telling.

I studied, read, and drank it all in. Listening to PaulisCatholic.com, I heard the book of Romans taught from an entirely new perspective. Wow! The pieces were all coming together now. My head was buzzing like a beehive with new concepts. Late one night, God's merciful kindness visited me as I lay curled up on a couch under a big blanket, being cyber-fed by Catholic websites, enraptured by all of this new teaching. I was listening to a podcast on "Infused Righteousness/Sanctifying Grace"—a Catholic teaching. When I heard what Catholics believe, I found it so beautiful, loving and transformative. "Infused Righteousness" means that God doesn't just love me because of what Jesus did for me on the cross, as amazing and profound as that is and as undeserving as I am. At Baptism, I am literally *infused* by Him and His Spirit so that I too may be made *holy*! Me! Holy! I, physical me, have a part in it. Me—the human me. God is able to do this because there is something good in me to begin with… because He made me in His image. His righteousness has something to "stick to"—to permeate. Of course, it's all by His grace, as He is always the source of all holiness. Church teaching has always stated this.

When I first heard this concept, it was as if I felt a beautiful injection of love enter my body and soul. For the first time I did not feel shiny on the outside and dirty beneath a holy veneer. I was elated to know that He cleansed *me* from the inside out by permeating both my *physical body* and my *soul* with His presence! And He delighted in doing it! I realized that I could be holy, as He is holy, and that there were and are holy people. I became very curious about the saints and especially the "incorruptibles," which, of course, I knew little to nothing about. What little I did know was wrong. I thought that they were wax dummies, not holy people preserved by God to be witnesses to us of His prominence in their lives, which, of course, they are!

It thrills me to this day to realize that God is doing something in me, not just because I am covered by Jesus' blood that cleanses me from all of my sin, (which I am) but also because He loves me because *I* am His... *all* of me is HIS—the good and the bad, the spiritual and the *flesh*…all His. And He loves me.

The Lord is complete and whole (Shalom) all by Himself-- absolutely complete, lacking in nothing. He does not *need* me to participate in my salvation, but He *allows* me to participate with Him because He knows *I* need it. It is as if God is a complete circle, completely whole. And because of His grace and love for me, He allows this Circle of Him, at His very heart, to be pierced and invites me to enter. He invites me to share in His sufferings and His joys by uniting all of mine with His. He invites me to learn of Him in ways I could never learn of Him unless I was a part of Him. I began to understand the mystery of hiding in the wounds of Christ and the Sacred Heart. They are inviting us in…I never had felt that before. I had never felt accepted and invited in, just as I was.

Because the Lord is *in* me, and I am *in* Him, He is not just *covering* me. I can be *totally* transformed--*all* of me.

The verse Philippians 2:12b,13 now became clear: "...work out your salvation with fear and trembling. For God is the one who, for his good purposes, works *in* you both to desire and to work." I am asked to join Him in this good work, to be His partner, His bride. We are ONE...mind, soul, spirit, *and body*. I am not working out my salvation... *We* are! And it is a process and a joy. As I take Jesus in daily in the Eucharist, I join in a wonderful wedding feast of love, The Lamb's great supper, that gives me His strength to enable me to do "...all things through Christ who strengthens me." (Phil. 4:13)

All of this new revelation was stirring in my heart a longing for physical contact. Sitting before the Host in Adoration was not enough for me. I wanted to be one with God in this beautiful and intimate way. I longed to touch, hold and be with God. He is real and He is physical. For my entire life, I had felt like He was my best Friend, only we had never actually met face to face. It was more like we had spoken on the phone daily for years. Now I had the chance to be actually, physically one with Him. He was starting to work on me and in me, infusing my soul with His presence, and I wanted to make it complete by taking the Eucharist into my being.

But imagine my heartbreak when I thought of all of the obstacles that stood in my way. I knew what joining the Catholic Church would do to my family relations, friendships, and to the ministry I had started by God's grace and been a part of for twenty years. Those very few who now knew of my journey were starting to ask questions, to look at me differently, and "get worried for me."

I sat in the Adoration Chapel day after day and prayed. I implored Him earnestly to show me my path so that my life could be lived for His Glory. "Lord, which road am I to walk? Show me the way! What do You want me to do? "

One day, I sat before the Blessed Sacrament, as I had so many times before, and miraculously, He enabled me to have another very real experience with Him. As I sat there, I was given a picture of a beautiful rugged mountain. There were enormous, jagged boulders going up the side of the face, but worn into them was a smooth, deep pathway. Climbing this pathway were pilgrims clothed in coarse white robes. As they climbed, the pilgrims veered off onto slightly smaller paths. At the end of this first "cul de sac," Mary was there to greet them. She would welcome them with a very warm smile and embrace them in her beautiful mantle. The pilgrims would not want to leave because her arms were so loving and her robes were so warm and soft, but she would kiss them and then point them upward to the top of the mountain where an empty Cross was visible. Being obedient and full of renewed strength, the pilgrims would return to the original path and continue their march upwards. There were several of these side paths and at the end of each was a saint waiting to embrace, strengthen and shoo them back on their way. Each pilgrim was so resolute in his or her mission. And each was climbing upward to the Prize, Christ Himself, waiting at the top.

I was so amazed at what I saw. It was beautifully clear. I could smell the trees and see the sandy grit that was beneath their feet as they shuffled up the path over the stones worn smooth by thousands, perhaps millions, of pilgrim feet. And then I saw the whole vision from a distance again, as from a bird's eye view. I asked the Lord, "What is this?" and He said, "This is the Ancient Way. You are to walk in it."

**Praise:** I praise and thank You for: "This is the Ancient Way. You are to walk in it."

**Prayer:** O Lord, let me never fear one more step that leads me closer to You. Give me strength to persevere and courage to continue on, even in the midst of the unknown. Open my heart and my mind to new things, even things that would change my life forever if only I would but trust in You. Keep me always seeking, always climbing upward, always upward to You.

**Promise:** "Fear is not in love. Instead, perfect love casts out fear..." 1 John 4:18

**Proof of the Promise**: I have learned that when I pray for an open heart and mind, Truth is revealed. If it is truly of God, it is good, and there is no need to fear.

**Ponder: Journal here** about the struggles that prevent you from taking another step toward God. Most struggles are seeded in fear. Fears of family or friend's reactions? Fear of the unknown? Fear of commitment? Along with prayer, what are other things

that you can actively do to help alleviate your fears?
Talk to God about this...

## Chapter 5

*I urge you, brethren, by the mercies of God, to present your bodies a living and holy sacrifice, acceptable to God, which is your spiritual service of worship. Romans 12:1*

*As my love for the Lord grew, so did my desire to trust Him and His ability to work mightily in my life. But how could I, so little and inconsequential, show Him--the God of the Universe-- that I trusted Him and believed in His power to act in my behalf? I prayed for guidance and I heard His answer loud and clear...*

## Metamorphosis

It is still hard to believe that, even after the latest revelation by God, I had doubts about whether I was to actually convert to Catholicism or remain in the Protestant church. I continued to walk in the practices I had learned from my spiritual director—those of Adoration, meditation using scripture, journaling, opening myself up to new and life-giving teaching, and physical exercise. I feared much, but I longed for the Eucharist, and to be a part of the Catholic Church.

During this period, I received a phone call from a beloved family member. She had been struggling with a form of addiction for many years and had at last made the decision to enter into a treatment program. I was thrilled beyond words, as our family had been praying over this intention for as long as I could remember. She told me that there would be a time during the course of the program when loved ones could visit to come and encourage her and to be encouraged. I was asked to go but, as I lived very far away, I was unable to go when the time came. However, I told everyone who was going that I would fast and pray while they were there together. I would ask God to intervene and bring revelation and true change.

Now let me say, when I said I would "fast" I really meant "struggle and complain" as I *loved* to eat… a lot. I had been praised for my cooking and enjoyed every part of the process—finding new recipes, buying and trying foods, and actually cooking. It was my hobby really. I even went to a few cooking classes, but of course, consuming the fruit of my labor was the best part. Sadly, my five-foot-one and three-quarter-inch frame did not agree. I was overweight by about forty pounds. I had learned to "live with it," though I really hated myself each time I got dressed. I had read on a funny cocktail napkin, "If you can't lose it, decorate it!" and that had become my motto.

When promising to fast, I genuinely meant that I would pray for my dear companions as they went to visit, but three days seemed like an eternity to not eat. I began to pray. And I prayed and prayed. I prayed for the situation and everyone and everything involved. I drank only water and fruit juice from sun up to sun down, and in the evening I would have a tiny portion of protein and a very small salad—really just enough to keep up my strength to serve my family's needs.

It was such a struggle. It was a battle of the wills. Sadly, I thought more about food than I did about God during those three days. But as the hours began to pass, something started to change in me. Things were becoming clearer. I did not actually perceive it until two things happened.

As I was praying for my family member, "Show her how much she needs You to fill her and enable her to get control in her life," God got my attention. I heard something very funny…I heard God clearly say, "Why don't you look in the mirror, honey?"

I was shocked! Me? This is NOT about me! This is about her and her unchecked urges and her inability to control herself. I dismissed this nudge from the Lord thinking that, after two days of fasting, I was starting to lose it! I turned to my email to distract myself.

It was then that I was truly convicted. My spiritual coach sends out a daily email message of encouragement to everyone on his list of over two thousand people. That day's email, I was quite sure, was intended for just one person on that list... me. The email asked some very innocuous questions that went something like this... "Do you do all things well and with the pure motive of pleasing the Lord when people are looking, and even when they are not looking?" I thought, "Well, most of the time... especially if they are looking... so I'm at least fifty percent on that one."

Next question: "Do you equally serve with a pure heart both those you love and those you don't love?" I thought once again, "Well, I sure serve those I love, at least when I feel like it...I guess I need to work on the other part... so again, about fifty percent on that one, too."

Feeling rather smug at my average score, I began to read the third and final question. This question could not have hit me harder if it had been shot out of my computer like a cannonball. I was about to be sucker punched right into the center of my soul..."Do you do things with moderation, self-control, and detachment?" "Huh!!??? Where is this coming from?" I thought. Why did he have to ruin my perfectly good track record with *that* question? Moderation?! Self control?! Detachment?! Oh my goodness! I am fasting for someone else to have these things, not me! I am a BIG FAT ZERO on all of these!" This was no coincidence! First the "mirror" comment, and now this email!

You see, I had never really seen any of these virtues as attractive or attainable. My father, whom I loved and admired dearly, had issues, I am quite sure, stemming from growing up during the depression years. My childhood had been punctuated by episodes of great excess followed by periods of great regret. He would purchase enormous heaps of things, most of them for other people, as he had a very generous heart. If he saw it, and it was a good deal, and he could afford it, he bought it (and sometimes lots of it!). When it came to food, the last course of every meal was a bottle of antacid passed around the table for anyone who had overdone it. He always partook. Unfortunately, I had grown up thinking moderation and self-control were optional—for amateurs, really. I was a Texan, for heaven's sake! Bigger was *always* better. And to be honest, I was not quite sure what "detachment" was, especially not in the Biblical sense.

So there I was, sitting, starving, and now feeling like I had been weighed in the balance and had come up short (or heavy, depending on how you looked at it). What to do? As God always has it, He never intends for spiritual truths to be just for or about one person. They are always for the whole body—His Church. He did not intend only to help my family member by my fast. He intended, if I was willing, to heal me, too.

I knew what to do. If I needed healing and God wanted me to have it, all I had to do was to throw myself on His mercy and ask for His help. So I did. But to my horror, the conversation did not go as I thought it would.

"Dear Lord, here I am again. You know that it is quite ironic that I have been praying for all of these things for others, when I was really in need of them myself. Thank you for opening my eyes to see that I am in need of Your healing touch in my own life. I know that You know that I have zero self-control, and so I ask You now to please help my efforts of self-control. Thank you for hearing me and answering me. In Jesus' name, Amen." What I heard in answer to this prayer left me stunned…

"No! I will not help you."

"WHAT?!" I asked in shock. "But You *have* to! I am Your beloved daughter and I need You! Where else can I go? What shall I do!?"

"If I help you, it will still be *your self*-control. It will be tainted by you, and will still be *your* efforts. But here is what I will do; if you will give me all of your utter lack of self-control, I will give you all of My control. It will be 'God-control' not *self*-control. Do you want to take this offer?"

"Wow! Yes! I would be a fool not to! I give You me… and You give me, You!? That is the best deal in the world! Of course! Yes! I take it" I said.

"And to show you I mean it, I would like for you to fast for seven more days, a total of ten days to prove to you it is *ME* who is at work in you, and not *you* doing it yourself."

Gulp! Seven more days!? How on earth? I was already peeling the paint off the walls to try to make it to three! How could this ever be possible? But I said, "Yes, Lord. Only by Your grace, mercy, and power working in me could this ever happen."

And so I did. And, believe it or not, it was easy. I had never experienced anything like it before. It was all Him. Anytime I was even slightly tempted to eat something I would say, "The old me would want to eat that and give in to temptation, but the new me will not, because it is not me at all, but Him who controls me by His grace, mercy, and love." *We* were able to successfully finish the fast and *We* were even able to exercise during it. *We* were never faint or even weary. He renewed my strength like the eagle, [Isaiah 40:31] and showed me many things during this time period.

A good friend asked why I was fasting. My answer was, "Because He did." Something in the fasting makes this material world shrink away to reveal truths on a deeper level. It is as if the ocean tide washes out and I can clearly see all the shells that are left on my beach. I know that fasting can be used in many ways: as a means of reparation for others; as a means of a reminder to pray for a special intention; as a means of God revealing to you what He would like to show you in your own life. That is what God chose to do for me- show me where I was most in need of Him and His freeing power. And ironically, it was in the same area of self control- or lack there of- that I was praying for Him to strengthen in another. While my addiction was not the same as hers, mine was controlling me, just as hers was controlling her.

By God's grace, I became very aware of how much I ate and when I ate. I realized I ate for many reasons, not just for fuel for my body. I ate when I was sad. I ate when I was happy. I ate when I was stressed and I ate when I was bored. I ate when I was cleaning up, even if I was stuffed. I ate to be social and I ate when I was lonely. I pretty much ate all the time. God showed me that what He made was good, but I was not using it properly. I was using it to take the place of Him in different times and ways. I prayed multiple times daily to turn my life over to Him in every way and I asked that He would take control, not me. I realized that in Galatians 5:21, when the fruits of the Spirit are named, "self-control" is listed last…maybe because it is the hardest one of all, not for God to give, but for us to receive. To hand it over, giving Him total control of our lives, our appetites, even our "learned" behavior is difficult.

I soon became aware that there were all different types of fasting, not just from food. My spiritual director suggested something called "spiritual fasting" where I was invited to focus on periods of time—hours or days—to specifically fast from my pride. This was equally challenging, but by God's grace, He would always reward the work that we would do together. I heard a priest once say, "God just cannot resist an act of faith!" And so, in my little acts of faith, reaching out and up to Him by fasting, He would show me new things and take me to higher degrees of trust in Him and docility to His will.

While it was never the goal of my fasting, but because God was showing me where I was substituting food for Him, once HE took control, I lost forty pounds over the course of the next year. I became more aware of my need to trust in God to "comfort" me, not food. It was the first time in my entire life that I was not "on a diet" or constantly thinking about food. I began to gaze at Him more and more, taking my focus off of eating. In a restaurant it became clear to me that I was consuming too much if I cleaned my plate. I noticed that my husband, who was six-foot-two inches and weighs two hundred pounds was given the same portion I was given. I started the habit of taking half of everything I was served home to be eaten later, as a sacrifice. At the house, I served myself the same meals everyone else ate, but I gave myself a smaller half-portion. I never felt "denied," except in my portion size, since I ate the same things that I always had, just much less of it. I continued to exercise daily, offering this up as well, and really began to look forward to it as a time to be with God, worshiping and praising Him for my ability to run, walk, or just get out and move, as there are so many who cannot. I would jog a block, then walk a block, until I slowly worked my way up to a nice long run. I was being transformed inside and out.

One day as I sat meditating on an antique butterfly collection that my husband and I had purchased at a flea market, I could not get over the beauty of these creatures: their wings, a riot of color tiled by iridescent microscopic scales. They had once been caterpillars, worm-like, creeping along, earthbound, and now here they were in all of their glory.

"How? What had made them change?" I asked.

"Me." He said. "And I am doing the same work in you. They do not struggle to change, they just let Me do it. They have total docility to My will."

"Metamorphosis of my soul?" I asked.

"Yes." I heard with a smile in the Voice.

**Praise:** I thank You for showing me, "…I am doing the same work in you. They do not struggle to change, they just let Me do it. Total docility to My will."

**Prayer:** Oh Lord, I pray that I will be completely docile to Your will. I give you all of me, and I pray that You, in exchange, will give me all of You. Take me and change me, from the inside out. Make Your desires, my desires. Give me "God control" in place of my "self control." I want to keep my eyes on You and off of the things of this world. I want to mount up with wings… and soar the heavens with You. Only by Your grace, mercy, love and power will this happen. Come, Lord, and fill me now I pray. Amen.

**Promise:** "So if anyone is a new creature in Christ, what is old has passed away. Behold, all things have been made new." 2 Corinthians 5:17

**Proof of the Promise:** I have learned that when we are docile and cooperative with His revealed will, true transformation will come.

Revelation (God to me) + Cooperation (me to God) = Transformation

**Ponder:** Everyone has weaknesses, and the enemy can exploit a weakness and turn it into his stronghold -- an area of your life where your self control is not enough!

**Journal here** about any strongholds in your life that you need to relinquish to our Loving God in order for Him, along with your cooperation, to transform them. Ask Him for the strength to be docile to His transforming power. What do you think of the concept of "God-control" versus "self control"?

## Chapter 6

*Trust in the Lord with all your heart and lean not on your own understanding; in all your ways acknowledge him, and he will make your paths straight. Proverbs 3: 5-6*

*God's timing is always perfect. He chose to introduce me to "His Special Someone" at the moment I would be most receptive, although at the time, I did not realize it. This stumbling block became my stepping stone...*

## The Stoplight

God did amazing things in and through the ten-day fast—things that can be described as none other than life-changing. He had my full attention now and He kept it in the most tender of ways. My heart, soul, mind, and body were held voluntarily captive by a God so loving, so gracious, and so powerful. How could I dare glance away, even for a moment? For the first time in my life I felt as if He was truly in control, and it was an "out of this world" feeling. It is, however, with a bit of hesitation that I write what happened next.

At the end of the fast, I was not only elated that *We* had made it, but a bit sad that the fast had ended. I had reached a state of euphoria, feeling like a balloon barely tied to this earth. I thought that, if the tiny string broke, I would just float off into heaven.

On the very last day, I was to go for one of the series of Catechism classes that my spiritual director, Fr. Michael, had arranged for my friends and me. The topic was Mary, and I was not really looking forward to it. As a Protestant, revelation about Mary was the Church teaching I found most difficult to accept. The timing, of course, was heaven-sent. Due to the fast, I was now wide-open spiritually, as if God had taken celestial pliers and pried off the lid to the jar of my soul. It had been super-glued on for so long that only an act of extreme grace could move it, but "POP!"— off it had finally come. The stronghold of "*self*-control" had been swallowed up by "*God*-control."

I drove, very carefully I might add, to my class. The only thing I was looking forward to was telling Fr. Michael about the stupendous things God was doing for me. Instead, after a quick handshake, my classmates and I sat down immediately, and Fr. Michael began his teaching on the Blessed Mother. I listened as best I could.

He began with the fact that Mary is called "Mother of God." "What a funny name," I thought. But he explained that because we believe the Trinity, the Father, Son, and Holy Spirit, though unique in their own identity, are also one, she could be called this. I understood his explanation, but it felt a bit funny, and I resolved to pray for God to open my heart to embrace this title more fully. I lingered on this a moment and concluded that this was really just a different way of looking at the relationship between Mary and God. I could see it was truth. She did give birth to Jesus, so it did make her "Mother of God" as well as "Mother of Jesus." Okay, so far so good.

"Ever Virgin" was the next title Fr. Michael explained. Roman Catholics believe that the Blessed Mother was not only a virgin when she conceived Jesus, but after she gave birth as well. I had heard one wise, old sage explain it "like sunlight streaming through glass, this is how the Virgin painlessly delivered Jesus and kept her virginity." I had been taught that Jesus had brothers and sisters, born to Mary and Joseph after the birth of Jesus, but Fr. Michael explained that, in the Bible, "brother and sister" are used also for close kin. Okay, I could see that. And I could even grasp the teaching that, since she had remained a virgin at conception, why could the same not be true *after* giving birth? I did believe that God could do anything, so why not this?

He then went on to explain that Mary intercedes for us from heaven. She had been taken up into heaven after her time on earth was finished, he explained. "Hmmm... well, she was not the only person in the Bible that had been whisked straight to heaven. There were Moses and Elijah, so why not Jesus' own Mother?" I thought.

Fr. Michael explained that, if we ask the saints to pray for us, they go directly to Jesus on our behalf, just as if we had asked a devout friend to pray for us about an issue. The only difference between saints and our friends on earth is that saints, like Mary, are now in heaven and closer to God and the ways and will of God, and therefore they make great advocates for us before Jesus and the Heavenly Father. Okay, I could understand that, too.

I had been doing so well, nodding in agreement silently to myself about all Fr. Michael was teaching us. But, just as with the email I had received at the start of the fast, I was blown out of the water by the next comment...

Fr. Michael began to explain that Mary was our best advocate because she was Jesus' Mother, (and who can say "No" to his Mother?) and because she had been *preserved from original sin in her Immaculate Conception. She was sinless...*

Whoa! That was it. I was finished! I absolutely could not embrace this teaching, not even if I had fasted for ten thousand years, I thought. All of my hopes and dreams of entering the Church just flew right out the window. I had hoped it would be my soul that took flight, since I had felt so buoyed by my fasting experience with God, but now, I felt totally deflated. It was as if this one comment was a tiny dart that struck my ballooned spirit and left me flat on the floor.

I spoke up and, with all sincerity, voiced my very contrary opinion: "I am afraid I am just fine with thinking of Mary as a sinful person, just like I am, who was filled with the Holy Spirit and gave birth to Someone so much bigger than herself, just like I am supposed to do." And at that point my ears and mind closed off, and I went inward to mourn the loss of all I had thought the Lord was calling me to be.

I began to recall what God had shown me during the fast—a very short and to-the-point-parable that was churned up again and again and again… in the funniest and strangest of places: "The kingdom of heaven is like treasure hidden in a field. When a man found it, he hid it again, and then in his joy went and sold all he had and bought that field" (Matthew 13:34). It had been so applicable to me until now. I was that guy! I had found The Treasure! It had been shown to me so clearly. The Eucharist! It was Him! Truly Jesus! He was my Pearl of Great Price! I was overjoyed! And I was beginning to feel I was to sell *everything* in order to buy the field and gain it. But this…? Oh my, how could I?

Surely God did not intend for *this* to be a part of all that I was to "acquire."

As I sat in the class, not hearing another word he said, I kept thinking, "Catholicism is a *huge* field I am going to have to buy into with *lots of things* that I don't really want or understand. I am wondering if I could just sell off the parts I don't want, and keep the parts I do want!? How on earth can I say 'Amen' to this?"

As I mentioned earlier, I believe that Fr. Michael noticed my disappointment. After class, he took me aside to ask what was wrong. I began to tell him about my irreconcilable struggle with this teaching. And then he said something that ignited a small glimmer of hope. He introduced the *Law of Graduality* which, as explained earlier, states that, if there is a teaching in the Church that you cannot grasp or accept at the present time, if you are willing to stay open to God showing you the truth about it, you can still become a Catholic. This was heavy teaching. It was frightening to me for reasons I could not explain. My world was turning upside down as I was beginning to see that there was probably a great deal more in the "field" of the Church that I would need to unearth over time. How could I take a leap of faith and buy the field, not knowing what lay beneath the surface of it all?

Fr. Michael assured me that there were great heaps of treasure, if I would only continue to be open to the Spirit and keep digging. He said God would show me more new things every day, but I had to resist closing the door and saying, "I could *NEVER* believe that." I needed to say, "Lord, I believe, help me in my unbelief."

I left the class much weightier than when I arrived. To make myself feel better, I decided to do what I had always done—to go shopping and to do it in a big way, as this was a BIG problem. Even though God had filled me with Himself so beautifully for the last few days, once my eyes were off of Him and onto my problems, I only remembered the former ways I used to make myself feel safe, secure, and loved. I would buy all that I had been missing for the past ten days— and do it in bulk.

As I drove to Costco, I was replaying in my mind the conversations and discussions in the class. I was thinking about how I felt about Mary and all that I had been taught to be true. I was asking God to help me. I was heartbroken and confused. I wanted Jesus so badly. I wanted Him in the Eucharist. But now this! To get to Him I would have to get past His Mother! Could I? I truly wanted to. I wanted to know the Truth and let the Truth set me free, but I was not sure of what Truth was. I began to pray, "Lord, show me the Truth. What is the Truth?"

As I came to a stoplight that was just like any other stoplight, I pulled up and, as I was the first car in the line of traffic, I gazed upward at it, so as not to delay when the light turned green. And then… there she was! I thought I must be seeing things. I squinted and thought, "What on earth?!" But I knew who she was the second I saw her. She was about seventeen and appeared very kind and sweet. She had on a brown dress and a blue mantle over her brown hair. She had a huge smile and her brown eyes sparkled as she spoke.

She simply said, "Don't let issues you have with me, keep you from my Son." And then she disappeared. I was stunned—absolutely speechless. I began to shake and pulled over as soon as the light turned green. I sat on the side of the road crying. I was overwhelmed by it all—God's grace and goodness during my fast and now this. Composing myself, I called Fr. Michael. At first, I did not want to tell him all that had transpired since I had last seen him, only a few minutes ago. I thought he would think I had at last lost my mind, or dismiss me for having too vivid an imagination, but he did not. He was kind and gentle and said something that made me feel so loved by God, not doubting my experience, but verifying it.

He said, "Oh Melissa, you are like Jesus' beloved disciple at the foot of the cross. He is giving you what He loves the most, His Mother."

**Praise** Mother of God, thank you for speaking to me! "Don't let issues you have with me, keep you from my Son."

**Prayer:** Dear Father, I have no idea what you may be up to. All I know is that You are all Good and all Truth. Please help me to be able to pray through all of my closed-mindedness—the red lights that stop my journey to You. Please change them into nothing but green, even the parts I most misunderstand and fear.

**Promise:** "His mother said to the servants, 'Do whatever He tells you.'" John 2:5

**Proof of the Promise:** I have learned that God can take our smallest effort of reaching out in limited faith, and use it for His great glory and our great gain if we are seeking Him with a pure heart. He will meet us where we are and bring us along closer to Him, if we remain open and stay close. The very humble Blessed Mother is always all about Jesus, and pointing us to follow after Him, we need not fear. We need to continue to pray for a pure, open and hungry heart for Him. And we must not let ANYTHING keep us from her Son, not her, not anyone… but most importantly not even ourselves.

**Ponder: Journal here** about how you feel about the Blessed Virgin Mary. Do you feel she is in competition with Jesus? Do you feel that she is our mother too? Do you have issues with her? Do you love her? Perhaps ask God to give you the same heart towards His mother, that He has...

## Chapter 7

*"There is no one holy like the Lord, indeed, there is no one besides You, nor is there any rock like our God. 1 Samuel 2:2*

*Our God is a jealous God. [Exodus 34:14] He surprised me by drawing me further away from all that I knew and was comfortable with...and deeper and deeper into Him. He now made it very clear that He did not just want a part of me, He wanted all of me...*

### The Rock

My beautiful Marian encounter taught me that there was a great deal more "treasure" to discover in the field of the Church than I had realized. Being an avid Bible reader and teacher, I was a bit skeptical that Catholic teachings were all biblically based. Much to my great relief, the more I studied and the more I applied myself, the more I began to see the biblical basis for Catholic truth—and the treasure just kept on coming.

I had spent my entire life reading and studying the Bible. It was not only my passion but had also become my identity. Although I was not an academic, I had been reading sacred scripture, commentaries, sitting under several great mentors, and teaching women for so many years that in some circles I was considered an authority of sorts on spiritual matters.

By God's grace, greater even than my head knowledge of scripture, was the zeal for it in my heart. I truly loved God and His Word, and for me, the two were inseparable. Telling people about Him through His Word was my greatest love; I was an evangelist down to the very marrow of my bones.

The library of our home was filled with biblical commentary books. I had inherited some from my grandfather, the Baptist minister, and I had spent umpteen dollars on maps, charts, diagrams, and models—anything to help me understand and make it come alive for those to whom I would try to explain it. I loved it—all of it. It was my pride and joy and the knowledge and love I had for it was such an integral part of my identity. *It* was me and *I* was it.

It became quite clear to me, that as great as my passion was for my books and sacred scripture, if I were to become a Catholic, much of my collection, and therefore my own personal "knowledge," would become obsolete. I would now become the student, not the teacher. Giving up my theology and my identity and becoming a very humble beginner once again was a daunting prospect. I had dreamed of going to seminary, and even recently had applied and was discerning a call to the priesthood through the Anglican Church. If I were to convert, all of this would be over.

But beyond this humbling thought was an even more horrifying realization... I would also need to buy a new and unfamiliar translation of the Bible. I loved my Bible. It was my "Sword" as it is called in Ephesians 6, and I could use it quite nimbly. When questions arose, I could, in a flash, find the answer. In the third grade I had the illustrious honor of being "The Sword Drill Bible Champion" of my Sunday school class. I had won my very own copy of a *Sword Drill Bible*, and I was very proud. And now...I would be fumbling even to find the right pages, and all of the scripture that I had memorized since age eight would be the "wrong translation"—not Church-sanctioned.

Along with my treasured books, I also kept in my library a fossil and mineral collection, and some other findings from nature: butterflies, bones, wasps nests, interesting plant matter, all things that reflected God and His creative genius. One day as I sat pondering my rocks, I felt the Lord nudge me and ask, "Melissa, would you give these to Me?"

"What, Lord? My rocks?" I asked rather puzzled.

"Yes," He said lovingly.

"Well…" I was a bit hesitant, as I *loved* my rocks. I had been collecting them since I was a child and they were a part of me—full of memories I relished. My father and I would hike into the hills of Texas and scramble up fresh-cut road passes, rough and crumbly, or creep over cliff edges to gather fossils and interesting mineral samples. We visited rock shops on just about every vacation, filling out the collection. I truly hated to give them up, but I thought, "It is *God* asking for them. He did make them. They are really His. I sort of just borrowed them so…I guess I should say, 'Yes!'" By a sheer act of will, I said, "Yes, Lord, You may have them."

And then He said, "What about your other collections… can I have them too?"

I looked around and thought, "Well, if He wants the butterflies, bones, and beehives, I guess that is alright as well, as they are also all His creations." So again, I said, "Yes, Lord, You can have those, too."

Then I realized that the Lord actually wanted something so much more dear to me than rocks or wings or feathers. He wanted something at the core of who I was. He wanted the books…no He wanted my

THEOLOGY. You see, I had used my theology like rocks, not only to build my life upon, but also to ashamedly chunk at people who did not agree with me. I had not always used my knowledge of Him and His word to lovingly build bridges or paths, but often as weapons to fire at my opponents…and sadly, I had a pretty good aim.

Now I realized, what He wanted. He wanted me! He wanted the very rock-bed of who I thought I was, who I had built and studied myself to be. He wanted all of what and who I had put my trust in… He wanted *me*. Could I give Him me in this way? The very core and identity of me? Could I give Him that too? Could I trust that He knew what He was asking for, and that He would not leave me de-constructed, alone, and hanging? Sitting on the small oriental carpet on my library floor, I cried, "If I give You *this*, I will have no idea who I am anymore."

And then I began to remember another wonderful revelation He had so lovingly shown me in the Adoration Chapel. It was of the mountain I had seen earlier. The mountain was large and rough and covered with huge boulders, just like before, only this time it was snowing and dimly lit. The pilgrims, as in the prior scene, were making their way up the smooth trodden path worn into the mountain facade. I could see them in their coarse, textured white robes. Up they went, single file, one behind the other, pointy hoods up, covering their heads from the snow. But this time, instead of seeing it from a distance, suddenly I was one of the pilgrims. I was shuffling up the mountainside. I was following the person in front of me. Then, without warning, the person I was following turned around so I could see His face. It startled me, but then my eyes focused and He was smiling a very warm smile. It was Jesus! He was in front of me! I then had an urge to look behind me, so I glanced backwards, and once again, it was Jesus! He was following behind me, too! "How astonishing!" I thought. He is before me and behind me! And then, as dreams and visions often do not make perfectly rational sense in the way in which they unfold, I was able to see myself from a distance, and yet I was also still on the path trekking upward. Looking at all of the faces on the path, I could see that they were all Jesus! "What could this mean?" And then I thought, "If everyone on this path has the face of Jesus…" With much trepidation, I was able to look upon my own face, and much to my great and very humbling surprise, it was Jesus' as well. I am almost unable to write of it, because I in no way want to equate myself to our Lord. But what I realized is this…it was Him all along, enabling me to sure-footedly make my way upward on the path of life—all of these years, in spite of bad weather or strenuous conditions, it was Him, all Him. He was surrounding, encouraging, filling, enabling—it was Jesus. My true identity was *Him*, not my theology, or anything else I could put my trust in, no matter how "good" it was. My truest core was not and is not me, but Him, by and through His Holy Spirit. And if I became a Catholic, that would still remain the same.

With this thought in mind, I was able to say, "Yes, Lord, You can even have my books, my theology, all of who I am. You can have me down to the very deepest center of my being, as I want nothing else to build my life upon, for You alone are my Rock."

And then I pictured in my mind's eye, gathering all of my books, and all of my rocks, and all of my other collections, and laying them out on the carpet for Him. And lastly, on top of it all, I laid my very beloved, marked up, dog-eared, coverless Holy Bible, which was my greatest material, earthly treasure, as my Bible represented all I knew and loved about Him…and I gave it to Him.

When I did, it was as if He took it all upward to heaven, a bit like Peter's vision of the sheet come down from heaven in the book of Acts. And with it, He took me as well! I felt completely swept up in love, as if I was going for a magic carpet ride. I was no longer earthbound. The core of my very being was tied only to Him in faith, and I trusted that He would guide and keep me safe, no matter what. And then, as suddenly as we went up, we came safely back to earth, right where we started from—my library floor.

A few days later, one of my friends handed me a beautifully wrapped package. It was rather heavy, and I was not sure what it could be. As I opened it, I began to laugh. It was a new Catholic Bible! It not only contained Holy Scripture but it had deep and insightful biblical commentary sandwiched in between each page—all that I would need to help me through my transition. Shortly after that, I received another—and another. I received several Catholic Bibles of different translations, all inspiring in their own way. The truth began to dawn on me...I had given the Lord my one Bible with sixty-six books in it, and He gave me several back with seventy-three books in each! Something I had known and now had become a reality to me was this: "You can never out-give God." God is certainly the most extravagant Giver!

**Praise:** Thank You God, Creator, that You prompted my answer to be "Yes" to "Would you give these to Me?"

**Prayer:** Most loving heavenly Father, Creator of all things in the universe, seen and unseen, including me, help me to trust in You to fill me and be my All. Let me not fear anything You would ask of me, even if You ask for the very core of my being! Please give me enough faith in Your great love and goodness, that I would happily give You all of me as You have given me all of You. Take me and make me into Your image, more and more each day. Amen.

**Promise:** The Rock! His work is perfect, for all His ways are just; A God of faithfulness and without injustice, righteous and upright is He. Deuteronomy 32:4

**Proof of the Promise:** I have learned that God will never ask us to give Him something that would be harmful to us, and if we yield, He will give us abundantly more in return than we ever had the courage to give Him.

**Ponder: Journal here** about what makes *you* -you? From where do you get your identity and your value? Is it from God? Do you trust God enough to place all of who you are in His hands and get all that you are from who HE says that you are...*His* beloved? [Col. 3: 12] Write to Him about this...

## Chapter 8

*Listen to counsel and receive instruction, that you may eventually become wise. Proverbs 19:20*

*As I was being drawn closer to the tender mercies of God, I felt I was nearing the point of no return. My heart was enraptured but my head demanded reassurance. I needed confirmation, and confirmation came just in the nick of time...*

### The Double-Take

At this point in the journey, I felt quite confident that God was asking me to trust Him—to take a leap of faith and convert to Catholicism. The Church calls it "Entering the Fullness of the Catholic Faith." Since I was already a baptized Christian, not converting from another religion, such as Buddhism, I would only need to be confirmed to become a Catholic. The question remained as to how, when, and where. I knew that this was not going to be easy for my family or my friends and that it would have great ramifications on my participation in the women's ministry that I had founded.

I had met Fr. Michael just before my own loving father became gravely ill and passed away. I could not help but think that the timing was providential since Fr. Michael was able to give me so much faith-based solace. At his suggestion, I had been going to St. Matthew's Cathedral to attend Mass and to sit and pray to mourn the loss of my dear dad. I was enraptured with the sheer beauty of it all. The church itself was magnificent. It was adorned with the most spectacular mosaics, all in the Pre-Raphaelite style, which happened to be my favorite form of expression in art. The entire place seemed to be a reassuring love letter from God to me. It was as if heaven was touching earth, and this place was a tiny crack in the door to my celestial Father's splendid home. It gave me great peace to imagine the happiness that my earthly father must have been experiencing in the fullness of His Presence. If I could have closed my eyes and conjured up an environment for me to sit and worship God where my spirit would be comforted and my soul would be touched by all of my senses, I could not have imagined a more perfect place. It was as if St. Matthew's had been built just for me.

I, of course, had been in dialogue with my husband, Dale, about all that was happening. I had not gone into every detail of my experience since I had some reservations about telling him what I felt God was calling me to do. I was not quite sure what his reaction would be. He had been supportive of my taking the Catechism classes and meeting with Fr. Michael, because he could see it was challenging me in new and, as of yet, unexplored ways in my faith. He could see the fruit in my life, as well. But I knew that my joining the Catholic Church would cause a real "hub-bub" in many ways, especially on Saturdays or Sundays, as I would need to attend Mass as well as our family church service.

After much prayer, I finally mustered up my courage to tell him that I was feeling a true calling to join the Catholic Church. In his most loving, devout, and pragmatic way, he said, "Well, Mel, if you feel God is calling you to become a Catholic, you had best do it, or that will be considered disobedience!" And he smiled.

I could not believe it! I was thinking to myself, "I wonder if he actually heard what I said!" He was so supportive. True, he had none of the "baggage" I had. He had not been raised in a particular denomination. His parents were kind and loving, but were not churchgoers. He had been raised overseas and had only become a Christian in high school through an interdenominational organization called "Campus

Crusade for Christ." He did not have all the hang-ups I did about unfamiliar beliefs. To him, if it was about Jesus, it was "all good," and it was just that simple.

He only made two requests: that I would first speak with the pastors at the Anglican Church where we attended, and, if given the "Okay," that I please wait about another year since he was on the Vestry (Board of Governors) of our church which was undergoing some tough transitions of its own. He did not want to further muddy the waters for anyone because of this. I agreed even though my heart so longed to take the Eucharist much sooner. I humbly and silently uttered a prayer, "Lord, You know my heart. Please change his as far as timing, if this be your will."

As Dale had asked, I quickly made an appointment to speak to one of the pastors at our church. Funny enough, he was a former Catholic himself. He was not only fine with my conversion, but quite delighted! He told me that people often came to him feeling this calling. What a relief! I then went to the heads of our healing prayer team to ask them to pray and discern if this was my true calling. Once again…surprise! The word was "Yes!" I was joining for all of the right reasons, and in the right way.

A few weeks later, on the one-year anniversary of my father's death, I asked my dear husband to please go with me to a Mass at St. Matthew's to pray for the repose of daddy's soul and to honor his memory. It was an absolutely perfect Sunday evening. The choir, the liturgy, the bells and smells—it was all there.

During Mass, my heart was full of sadness at the death of my father and, yet, at the same time, I was joyful because of the hope we have in Jesus. I looked at my husband and he so tenderly looked at me. I did not say a word. He then touched my hand and said, "Mel, I can tell…this is for you. You can join the Church anytime you feel you are ready. You do not need to wait."

Ahh! The blessing! The release! The joy! And at the same time… the fear! I had been given the "All-clear! Go ahead!" signal on every level and now it was up to me to follow through! I panicked! But I knew I had to follow through.  I would now need to inform my pastors at our church of my final decision, talk to my children, friends, and co-ministers in the Word.

First, I phoned Fr. Michael and gave him the great news. He was, of course, elated. Then I began in time to tell each one that would be affected by this change and, as one can guess, there were many varied reactions to the news—some surprisingly positive, others very hurt, shocked, even disappointed and angry.

As the weeks passed, I ashamedly not once, but twice backed out of the dates Fr. Michael had set for my Confirmation service. I was still just so afraid, and struggling with the potential fallout of my decision. Because I had taken the class with him and he knew of my struggles and theological journey, Fr. Michael had been able to arrange for me to come into the Church at my beloved St. Matthew's through a very kind priest there. At the time I was unaware of all of the complications he had faced to make it work. I knew nothing of the administrative details he had to arrange and the permissions necessary to do a Confirmation during the liturgical season of Lent. The priest at St. Matthew's had been accommodating, but poor Fr. Michael was more stressed than I realized. When I called the third time to tell him, that I was AT LAST READY to be Confirmed, he sweetly, but with a slight urgency in his voice, stated, "If you back out again, it will be beyond my ability to help you. Because of the Church calendar you will need to go through an RCIA program and wait another year to join. I need to let St. Matthew's know by 5:00 tonight if you *really* are going to go through with it this time."

His frankness about the situation helped me to realize I needed to make the decision once and for all and stick with it. I had to let my "yes be yes or my no be no." I knew that God had been so gracious to me already. Fr. Michael was literally pounding his head on his desk asking me, "WHAT MORE COULD YOU WANT? You have been given so many graces, consolations and signs!" To him, it was absolutely clear. And at times, it was to me, too. I knew it was what I was supposed to do, but I was just so full of fear.

A dear stranger at Mass one day had given me a prayer card, and I so wanted to mean every word of it… I just kept praying it day after day:

*Lord Jesus, I desire to receive You into my heart. Through this union with You I offer myself to the heavenly Father as a sacrificial host abandoning myself totally and completely to the most merciful and holy will of my God. From today onward, Your will Lord, is my food. Take my whole being: dispose of me as You please. Whatever Your Fatherly hand gives me, I will accept with surrender, peace and joy. I fear nothing, no matter in what direction You lead me. I no longer fear any of Your inspirations nor do I probe anxiously to see where they will lead me. Lead me O Lord, along whatever road You please; I have placed all my trust in Your will, which is, for me, love and mercy itself.*

(Adapted from St. Maria Faustina Kowalska's Act of Oblation, *Diary of St. Maria Faustina Kowalska: Divine Mercy in My Soul*, 1264).


Father Michael needed to know by 5:00! I began to pray once again for a final sign that would relieve my anguished heart and soul once and for all, and allow me to move forward into a life filled with peace with Him in the Catholic Church.

I am quite aware that asking for this final sign was possibly presuming on the Lord's patience, but I was aware that He knew my heart, and that He knew that it was all His. And yet, there was a raging war going on inside of my head that He needed to vanquish once and for all.

Just ten minutes shy of my "deadline," I had never felt such a tumultuous angst in my soul. I escaped from the noisy world into the quiet of my car to pray. The cherished silence was suddenly and surprisingly interrupted by the ringing of my phone. It was a number I did not recognize and the area code signaled it was from California. I was so deep into prayer, pleading to God for an answer that I was annoyed that I had forgotten to turn off my phone. I hesitated and wondered who it could possibly be and decided after several rings to take the call never even considering the possibility that this could be the answer to my prayer... The caller asked, "Is this Melissa?" I said, "Yes."

She said, "Hi! My name is Myrna, and I am a friend of Evans'. You called me about three months ago. I lost your number and just now found it. I felt I was supposed to call you back but I only have about ten minutes, because I am getting on a flight. How can I help you?"

I was shocked. Years before I had ever thought about becoming a Catholic, a friend of mine had spoken to me after one of my Bible study lectures. Her name was Evans and she had asked me if I had ever met a friend of hers named Myrna. When I replied "no," she said, "Well, you remind me so much of her. You talk alike, you teach alike, you have the same passion of spirit. And coincidentally, her husband's name is Dale, and her daughter's name is Melissa. You guys are so much alike it is uncanny. Only thing is... she became a Catholic."

I said, "Wow! Now that is weird. We sound so similar, but why would anyone want to do that?"

Fast-forward about ten years to the present moment. I had spoken to Evans and gotten Myrna's phone number because I very much wanted to speak with Myrna about her journey and why she had decided to become a Catholic. I had thought that, if Evans had said we were such kindred spirits, perhaps Myrna could answer some of my questions. The only problem was, I had never reached her. I had left a message and, quite frankly, had forgotten I had even called her.

"Thank you for calling me back," I said. "You pretty much won't believe the timing of your call and I, too, only have about ten minutes." I explained I was considering becoming a Catholic and then said, "If you don't mind, can we just cut to the chase and can you tell me what it was that made you decide to become Catholic? How did you know you were to do this?"

She began, "Oh, it was crystal clear. I was praying and the Lord gave me a vision of a mountain and it was covered with large boulders. At the top of the mountain was a cross. Along in the boulders was a path worn into the rocks by many thousands of pilgrims coming from all over the world streaming up the path. And then I heard a voice and it said, 'This is the Divine Way. You are to walk in it.'"

I could not believe my ears! I was stupefied. I said, "Could you please repeat what you just said?" She said it again, and then added, "Oh, and of course, in the Catholic Church I received the Eucharist, Mary as my mother, and all of the saints as intercessors...why would I not have wanted to join?"

I was utterly speechless. I simply said, "thank you," and hung up the phone.

To this day, I have never been so stunned. God in His absolute loving, merciful kindness gave me all I needed to hear and more. Myrna's vision was an almost exact carbon copy of the one He had given to me. How could I doubt that I was to join the Church for one more minute? Bolstered with extreme confidence, and humbled once again, I called Fr. Michael at the stroke of 5:00 and simply said, "I'm ALL in."

On February 27, 2010, I was received into the fullness of the Roman Catholic Church. I became Melissa Therese of the Child Jesus and the Holy Face. (I had fallen in love with St. Therese after reading *Story of a Soul,* and I couldn't help but think she had more than a little something to do with all that had taken place.) There were no lightning strikes, visions, or audible voices. There was only nervousness that gave way to an enormous lifting of a weight from my soul. I felt as if I had dropped a one-hundred-pound backpack off of my shoulders. At last I felt peace. I had a true sense that I had come home. The fight was over and the struggle had ended. There was a strong sense of grounding—of rock solid grounding. I had never felt like this before. I was completely whole... I had absolute Shalom.

And did it last? Well, yes, for awhile. At times, I honestly would look down to see if my feet were still touching the earth....they were. I so longed for the Eucharist. I would plan my day around when and where I could get to Mass, a bit like an alcoholic planning his day around a drink, only this was THE Spirit that was intoxicating my soul. It was a most euphoric time. Little did I know that God was filling me to the brim because I was about to be poured out like never before. This was the beautiful calm before the storms that were about to hit—and hit very, very hard.

**Praise**: I praise You Lord for the confirmation of hearing from Myrna, "This is the Divine Way. You are to walk in it."

**Prayer:** Heavenly Father, You are always working on both ends of the equation of my life. Help me to trust in You and Your timing. Please give me the grace I need to walk in FAITH even when I have no idea where the path or Your inspiration will lead. Help me to love You more, and to show that love through my obedience, even when I do not completely understand. Please, Lord, give me more of You in every way possible. Amen.

**Promise:** "A man's heart plans his way, but the Lord directs his steps." Proverbs 16:9

**Proof of the Promise:** I have learned that He has got us absolutely covered, and is weaving our live's paths always toward Him… if we will only listen, and follow closely out of love.

**Ponder: Journal here** about any encounters you have had with God. Sometimes, as you know, they can be like little bread crumbs He has strewn all along the way--"God-incidences" meant to encourage you. Other times the experience can be profound…

## Chapter 9

*Behold, I will bring to it health and healing, and I will heal them; and I will reveal to them an abundance of peace and truth. Jeremiah 33:6*

*I thought the Master Sculptor had finished chiseling for a while and that my soul was starting to take shape, but this was not the case. I still had a great deal to learn about the God of Love, and He literally stopped me in my tracks to teach the greatest lessons of all...*

## Mama Mia!

As I stated at the very start, the largest hurdle that kept me from the Catholic Church was the culture and doctrine pertaining to Mary. But thankfully, when she so humbly appeared to me and told me, "Don't let issues you have with me keep you from my Son," it seemed as if the logjam in my heart cleared, and my resistance toward her melted away. She no longer seemed threatening. As a matter of fact, I now considered her an ally. I had a "friend on the inside." After all, when my pride and misunderstanding kept me from Mary, she came to me. She sought me out humbly, tenderly, and authoritatively. The Lord had so beautifully softened my heart that I was now able to view her with eyes of love, not judgment.

During the Advent season leading up to my Confirmation, I was given a book called *The Reed of God* by Caryll Houselander. I had been reading snippets of her work in the *Magnificat* and was captivated by her writings. She was a true artist. This book was about the Blessed Mother and how we are to emulate her. I was fascinated.

Houselander's work became my soul's companion. She stated that we must have "Emptiness… That virginal quality…it is not a formless emptiness, a void without meaning; on the contrary it has a shape, a form given to it by the purpose for which it is intended…like the hollow in a reed, the narrow riftless emptiness, which can have only one destiny: to receive the piper's breath and to utter the song that is in His heart.

It is emptiness like the hollow in the cup, shaped to receive water or wine.

It is emptiness like that of the bird's nest, built in a round warm ring to receive the little bird...
(Our Lady) was indeed like those three things.

She was a reed through which the Eternal Love was to be piped as a shepherd's song.

She was the flowerlike chalice into which the purest water of humanity was to be poured, mingled with wine, changed to the crimson blood of love, and lifted up in sacrifice.

She was the warm nest rounded to the shape of humanity to receive the Divine Little Bird."

I was in love. I wanted to have this "emptiness." I wanted to be like Mary and make room in my life to be absolutely filled with Him.

The Lord put a longing into my heart to grow more deeply spiritual and so I felt determined to emulate Jesus and the Virgin Mary, following them all the way from Jesus' birth to His death. I would take this next year to read the Gospels, grasping Mary's hand with my one hand and Jesus' with my other. They would be my companions to show me new spiritual truths through their eyes.

It had become my practice since meeting with Fr. Michael to go daily to the Adoration Chapel. There, I would sit, read, and pray. One of the prayers I loved to lift to the Lord was the *Te Deum* printed in the back of the *Magnifica*t. The funny thing was, month after month, I had underlined the same line, over and over again, and I was really not sure why. The line states:

"When you became man to set us free <u>you did not spurn the Virgin's womb.</u>"

As I sat in the Adoration Chapel one day and prayed and offered my desire to the Lord to grow in holiness by accompanying Him from birth to death and back again, I distinctly heard these words…
"Not from My BIRTH to My death but from My CONCEPTION to My death."

Huh? That was funny. "What could that mean?" I thought.

That evening, in my home, after cleaning up the dishes from dinner and getting my little one to bed, I sat down for a rare moment of evening quiet. I just happened to pick up a coffee table book called, *Splendors of The Magnificat.* I opened to the introduction and there I read:

"The Magnificat belongs on the lips of all those who have been begotten from above by the power of the Holy Spirit and *in the waters of Mary's womb—a place that the saints identify as the locale where one is formed into the divine image of Mary's Son."*

Wow! In the Adoration Chapel I was told to emulate Him from conception to death, and now I had read this! I so longed to follow Jesus and His blessed Mother, but I had not even been aware of such a thought until this moment. (He) "did not spurn the Virgin's womb…"

But would I? Was I willing to make Mary my true mother, not my adopted mother, but my *real spiritual mother*? In order to do that, she would need to "give me birth."

After pondering and praying, I felt that, in this Advent season, I would go to the Adoration Chapel and prayerfully picture myself in Mary's womb with Jesus. I would picture us as twins! I tried to imagine what it must have been like for Him to leave the splendor of Heaven and to be confined in such a little space. The God who *created all* was now *being created*! He not only looked and acted like His heavenly Father (He is the exact representation of His nature [Hebrews 1:3], but was taking on human flesh, Mary's flesh, and would resemble His mother as well.

It was so sweet, and again, so humbling. Day after day, baby Jesus and I would just happily sit peacefully in Mary's womb together and she would sing and talk sweetly to us—just like I did to my babies when they were in my womb.

I emptied myself out and was being rebuilt in the womb of her love. I have never felt so loved, nurtured, and cared for. She was teaching me a new way of being kind and of self-giving. I was being enfleshed by her, to look like her…and like Him.

And then on Christmas, we were born! And at last, Mary was my Mother—my real mother—not my adopted mother, but my *real* mother. And best of all, I was hers. It was like in John 19:26… Jesus was saying to me, "Behold, your mother!"

You see, I have such a wonderful earthly mother; I never knew I needed a perfect spiritual mother. But just as I had a wonderful earthly father, I still need and needed a relationship with my Perfect Heavenly Father. God gives us all we need in the heavenly realm so that, when things fall short, as they inevitably do since none of us are perfect in the earthly realm, we can still be totally at peace.

Fast-forward into the new year. Within a few weeks, I became a Catholic. I was in a state of euphoria! I now had Jesus in the Eucharist, all of the sacraments, Mary as my mother, and all of the saints of heaven to pray with me and for me. I had Shalom! Earthly life was, in my opinion, as good as it gets… for about a week.

Life is neither "all great," nor "all horrible," and it seemed in these days to be a combination of both, simultaneously. Joys and sorrows are like railroad tracks that run parallel, at least in my life. I decide which track to gaze upon. If I gaze only upon the sorrows and sufferings that come my way, I get bogged down and "jump the track" so to speak. If I choose to look at Jesus, count my blessings, see the joy and the good things He brings alongside, even out of the sufferings, and constantly praise Him ("singing my way through life"), the journey is far smoother.

And so…shortly after my joyous entrance into the Church, we learned some very sobering news. My husband's darling sister who had Down syndrome and lived with us on and off throughout the year was diagnosed with a very aggressive form of melanoma. Cecilia came to stay in our home permanently and before too very long hospice care was needed. I now got to put into practice all I had been experiencing from the Blessed Virgin: kindness, patience, gentleness, and self-giving.

It was horrifying to see Cecilia in so much pain. Her cancer was not only internal, but had also spread over the surface of her poor little body. It was as though her skin was blooming melanoma blossoms, it was heartbreaking beyond all telling, almost beyond description. I cannot truly express what it was like. The tumors were in various stages and sizes—some as big as my hand. We had to clean and dress them often so that they would not get infected. It was almost more than I could bare to even look at them. She would cry and ask us for help. Her mental age was about that of an eight-year-old…it was like seeing and not being able to rescue a suffering child.

I am very squeamish by nature but I felt that the Lord and His beautiful compassionate mother enabled me to do things I could never have done alone. I pictured Cecilia as Christ lying there, and me as Mary, bathing her wounds. My dear husband was a rock. He never flinched. He so tenderly did all that was required each day. And the hospice workers who would come to check on her could not have been more kind and loving. God sent what we needed just when we needed it.

Cecilia passed very quickly, within only a few months, leaving a huge hole in our lives. She had taught us so much over the span of her lifetime about laughter and joy even in the midst of unkindness or deep suffering. She embodied the true beauty of a very child-like faith and unconditional love.

After her death, our lives went on, but it was a very difficult time. I was so thankful for all that the Church and my faith had brought to me—the disciplines Fr. Michael had instilled in me—daily Mass, Adoration, journaling, and exercise, all of which helped greatly to ease the loss of Cecilia. Those were now the "other rail" I focused on to keep me chugging along.

Before too long, led by God's grace and accompanied by an amazing group of fellow Catholic women, I felt inspired to begin a chapter of a Catholic women's Bible study called *Walking with Purpose* in my home parish. Margarita, Linda, and I were introduced to the program's founder, Lisa Brenninkmeyer, and God began to bless our efforts. Very quickly, the program grew out of that original study in my home parish to other parishes in our area, reaching hundreds of women. It seemed to me like life was finally getting back to normal.

But, once again, out of the blue, tragedy struck. Within a year, I myself would have an accident, experience a traumatic head injury, concussion, and spinal injury that alerted us to a pre-existing brain condition called a chiari malformation. The accident, combined with the chiari, caused me to be temporarily paralyzed, lose a great deal of both my short-term memory capability and the long-term fullness of mobility on my left side, and to experience paralyzing back and headaches. I had to lay flat in a darkened room with sunglasses, earplugs, and a neck brace for nearly three months. Never before had I experienced such trauma or needed Mother Mary like I did during that episode.

I had wonderful friends who ministered to me like angels. Linda brought me the Eucharist daily; it became my Oxygen and my Glue—it kept me whole. I had felt a bit like an egg which had been cracked open. The Eucharist and prayer were the means the Lord chose to hold me together and mend my poor fractured shell. Heidi organized prayer times and Kathryn arranged for meals for my family. I never could have made it without the Body of Christ, these friends were truly His hands and feet. I felt His love through each one.

Three different life-changing questions became a part of my healing process:

1. Fr. Michael Gilmary, a Maronite Monk, asked: "*Are you suffering well?*" I never knew that I could! But this became my goal! "Offer it up!" and "The only tragedy in suffering is wasted suffering!" became my mottos. I

united my sufferings to Christ's as a prayer for every intention He placed on my heart. I did not want my suffering to be wasted—not one minute of it.

2. I had heard a beautiful homily given while I had been caring for Cecilia. The priest had told the story of a tribe of Native Americans who instructed their young boys and girls, as part of an adult initiation rite, to "Look and see the hardships of our life and how we suffer. Until you learn to suffer, you will always be a little child in an adult's body." I felt as though I was learning how to suffer, and suffer "well." It was a great means of spiritual maturation for me. I often asked myself, *"What am I learning from this?"* so as not to miss "the good parts" God had in store for me through the ordeal.

3. Jane, a longtime friend offered: *"Ask God, 'What do You want to be to me in this situation that You could be to me in no other?'"* And so I did… He wanted to be my *"Everything,"* my *"Completer"* when I felt very "incomplete." Instead of looking at all I was unable to do and getting discouraged by it, I tried to see everything as a love note from God. I tried to look to see how He would "do it" in order to "complete me." He usually cared for me through friends or family, or sometimes would just give me the consolation of being able to be okay without it.

He, of course, had also given me her, the Blessed Virgin, my Mother. And there would be times that I would cry out to God and to Mary in pain, and I could literally feel her mantle of love wrap around me to bring me great comfort.

I was invited to apply to go to Lourdes, France, with the Order of Malta. The Blessed Mother appeared there in the 1850s and left waters that have become a site for pilgrims seeking healing. At the time I was so weak and woozy that I could not even think about going. After many months, when I was finally beginning to be able to walk a straight line again when the trip was only one week from departure, by God's grace, and I am sure, as a result of much prayer by friends, family and gifted prayer ministers I felt strong enough to make the journey. Miraculously a spot opened up, and off I went.

On our first day at Lourdes, we entered the baths, and I was, quite frankly, overwhelmed, freezing, and scared to death. I could sense in my spirit that it was a very powerful place, but for many reasons, when I entered the frigid water, I was not prepared for what would take place next. As I stepped down into the icy waters, I suddenly felt an influx of heat down my back and on my left side. Something miraculous was happening. I felt I was being healed but I was so fearful that I asked "what ever it was" to *stop* until I could understand better all that was taking place… and so… it did. I was then asked by the assistants there if I wanted to kiss the statue of the Blessed Virgin that was placed at the end of the bath. I said, emphatically, "NO!" All I wanted was to get dressed and get out of there!

My lower back was now pain free and I could feel, for the first time in what seemed forever, in perfect alignment. My headache was gone, too. It was a marvelous feeling after months of pain. But my left leg was still as weak as it had been before. I got back to the hotel and was quite shaken. I was searching for a lifeline so I called a couple who were long-time friends—my spiritual mentors. They happened to be Protestants involved in a healing ministry, and had taught me a great deal over the years. I told them where I was and what had happened... and, once again, God was *full of surprises*! I did not expect to hear what they had to say.

Their best advice to me was to go back to the baths and try again! They told me that the enemy *hates* the Virgin Mary. In Genesis 3:15 it states that she was prophesied to crush the head of the serpent, and in the book of Revelation Chapter 12 the devil is portrayed as the dragon who tried to devour her and her Child Jesus, but Mary was victorious in the end! So this time, they counseled, I was to ask the Virgin to *simply step on the head of anything inside of me that was not from God!* Gulp! The last thing I wanted to do was to go back into that water! I dreaded it for the rest of the trip.

On the last day we were given a chance to go again. I went with fear and trembling—literally! But this time, it was an entirely different scenario. I ended up accompanying a friend's child, so we were put into the children's section. (Unless you become like little children... Mt. 18:3) I once again felt the nurturing care of the Blessed Mother. This time, instead of

114

wanting physical healing when I stepped into the water, I simply stated, "I want you to crush whatever is not of God inside of me and I want whatever YOU want!" And when I put one foot in, my entire life began to flash before my eyes, and I saw all of the injustices and indignities that I had experienced as a child and growing up.

I had a sort of "righteous anger" burning in me all of my life, but I never exactly knew its source, and at last, here it was—I could see it. And when I did see it, I saw something so amazing happen to it! The beautiful and powerful foot of the blessed Mother came crashing down on the head of the serpent and KILLED IT and then RELEASE! It was gone! Miraculously all of this pent up fury and frustration was gone! I had peace and joy like I had never had before! I had a powerful and capable Mother, and I did not even know I needed her! She conquered what I could not, to set me free to love.

This inner healing I experienced was so much more essential than the physical healing I initially pursued. Praise be to God, as the years have passed, I have experienced a great deal of additional physical healing due to God's grace through prayer and my wonderful physical therapists Joe and Michael who helped keep me upright and moving. God uses all types of healing methods in our lives, but God knew what I needed at the time, and He brought it to me through the loving hand (or foot!) of the Blessed Virgin.

And this time, when they asked me if I would like to kiss the Virgin statue at the foot of the bath, I said, "YES!" and I gave her a huge kiss! My wonderful, humble, kind, conquering, and powerful Mother! My heavenly Mother of whom I had been so ignorant.

I now know that we have the *perfect heavenly family*, and if we are cooperative and allow all the goodness that is them to flow through us, God allows us to give adequate grace to all of those who are less than perfect here on earth, because we don't *need* them to be perfect. They can be human, *just as we are human,* and we can forgive each other's trespasses and failures and inadequacies.

God has given us all we need to make it through this life victoriously. We need only give ourselves to Him with confident abandonment, and then look with great surprised delight at His handiwork in and through our lives. He has many means to accomplish His great work.

**Praise:** Bless you, Lord of life. "Not from My BIRTH to My death, but from My CONCEPTION to My death."

**Prayer:** Lord, please give me the grace to be willing to be formed by the Holy Spirit in the womb of Mary, just as Jesus was, so that I can be like Him and like her in all ways. Mother Mary, please crush the head of anything in me that is not of God the Father. Please untie all the knots of my past sins and the sins of others that entangle and enrage me. I want to have more fully the fruits of the Holy Spirit: love, joy, peace, patience, kindness, goodness, faithfulness, gentleness, and self-control. Please grant me the fortitude I need to press heavenward, as maturation is a process, sometimes even a struggle, and it can take a lifetime! Grant me patience with myself. Amen.

**Promise:** "I will put enmities between you and the woman, between your offspring and her offspring. She will crush your head, and you will lie in wait for her heel." Gen 3:15

**Proof of the Promise:** I have learned that Mary is our humble, gentle, but also powerful and capable mother. She is able to crush the head of the serpent of all that is in us that is not of the Father. I need only to ask her to do it. For more about Mary's ability to "mother us" through every trial, see Appendix 2.

**Ponder: Journal here** about any knots that the Blessed Mother may need to undo, anything that keeps you from living a life of true freedom. Perhaps take a look at your "sufferings" and see if you are "suffering well" and offer them up to our Loving Lord so that you may be more united to Him in His suffering. Finally, ask the Lord to show you what He wants to be to you now, right where you are, that He could be to you in no other time or place due to your circumstances, and speak to Him about this...

JESUS ROBBED OF HIS GARMENTS

## Chapter 10

*For he looks to the ends of the earth and sees everything under the heavens. Job 28:24*

*"Near-sighted" describes me in more ways than one. Even in a spiritual sense, I don't see well beyond my own limited experience. Accompanied by the Lord on this life's journey, however, I know He sees everything, not just what's next! He sees and remembers--every tear, every sorrow, every joy, every moment. And once in awhile He reminds me of this in the most tender way...*

## The God Who Sees (Gen 16:13)

I am, quite interestingly, writing this from the place where it all began, in that very canyon in Texas where God wounded my heart with love for Him—a wound I received as His child, and from which I have happily never recovered. Many times I have returned to drink the water that flows so freely here from the rocks, and each time He has lovingly met me under the wide arms of the enormous star-filled sky.

It has been more than eleven years since this journey began, if you count the initial inspiration of the Eucharist on the rocky path up where the bluff meets the clouds, up in that very "thin place." (That is the Celtic expression of where the distance between heaven and earth collapses and one can most easily be transformed into one's better self.) But in actuality, it has been fifty years… my lifetime thus far, step-by-step, little-by- little, inching along, sometimes feeling as if I were being dragged along by the hand, as the angel of the Lord did for Lot in Genesis 19 to get him to where he needed to be.

I have had time to think and rethink all that has taken place. I believe that, unlike what I was taught as a child, in so many ways mainstream Catholics and Protestants are not so different, in fact, not different at all in what they fundamentally believe. Pope Francis has been very instrumental in pointing out our shared heritage, and helpful in building bridges, in that respect. And, of course, there are deeply rich ministries out there like *Alpha* that take what marks us as Christian, the foundational truths that can be applied to all, and present them in an engaging way so that they become life-giving and truly transformational for anyone. Fr. Cantalamessa, preacher to the Papal household, wholeheartedly believes in *Alpha*. I have been a part of this wonderful ministry for years and, although it originated with the Protestants, delightfully, at present more Catholic Churches are running it worldwide than Protestant churches. For more information see: www.alphausa.org

One of the many beautiful things I have learned from *Alpha* and from years of being a part of the Protestant Church and a women's Bible Study is the power of the small group experience. Most Protestant Church cultures excel in this, meeting together for intimate home groups or Bible Studies. This is something that the Catholic Church is beginning to appreciate--the beauty and need for small group study as a powerful tool for evangelization and personal transformation.

My greatest joy is to share my faith experience with others. I believe that God meant for my faith to be *personal*...but never *private!* God is Community—the Trinity. He knows we thrive in community and we are told to "Speak to one another in psalms, hymns and spiritual songs…" [Ephesians 5:19] meaning that we are to get together and talk about Him, and share the great and worthy things He is doing in our lives and to encourage each other in our daily struggles. We are to learn about Him and from Him in the scriptures.

Recently, Pope Francis urged the faithful to read the Gospel every day, to carry it in their pockets, to keep it on their bedside table, "because reading the Gospel is what brings us joy." We are to embody the old catechism adage of "Discover and Share!" The sharing is what makes my faith come alive, because God loves to speak to me, not only through His Word, the sacraments, His priests, and prayer, but also through *others*. That is why it is so important that "We should not stay away from our assembly, as is the custom of some, but encourage one another…" [Hebrews 10:25]. We must share our life experiences, the ways in which God has touched us and taught us, because we never know how God will speak to us or through us to someone else.

As I mentioned earlier, even though I was taught by some as a child that Catholics were not like us and that the Church was evil, God kept His eye on me. When I was still very young, too young to be taught the difference between "them" and "us", I watched a movie that turned my heart toward God and prepared me to think of the Church in a different way. The Spirit mysteriously chose to work on my tender little soul through a Hollywood film. I saw *The Trouble with Angels* with Rosalind Russell, and decided that I, too, should become, of all things, a very unlikely "sister" like Hayley Mills. After several days of pondering the call, I mustered up my courage and decided to announce to my family my "scathingly brilliant idea!" as Haley Mills would often say throughout the movie. I chose an odd moment for my declaration. We were leaving for a family vacation to visit my grandparents and, once the station wagon was tightly packed and we had all found our appointed places among the suitcases, blankets, and travel board games, I boldly blurted out that I felt I was to "take the habit" and become… a nun!

Well, as one can imagine, my deep conviction was met, not with the sort of delight I had hoped for, but with a different kind of delight—side-splitting laughter as my parents and sisters tried to explain to me that we were *Baptists*, not Catholics, and Baptists *don't have nuns*! They told me that I could become a missionary or an evangelist, and that is exactly what I have endeavored to do in my life —to spread His love through the study and teaching of His word. But at that time, I was crushed, and I buried my head in my pillow and wept bitterly in the back seat of the car all the way from Houston to Dallas—the longest five-hour drive of my life. I knew, even then, however, that God saw my childlike faith, and that somehow, if a Baptist could be a nun, I was all His. I was giving myself to Him, and I knew that He would honor my simple, and, what seemed to others to be ridiculous, offering. God collected my tears and, as it says in Psalms 56:8, "Kept them all in a bottle."

Forty- plus years later, as I sat in my little parish in Georgetown, preparing to pray one of my new and rich Catholic practices, the Stations of the Cross, my pastor came into the Church. He approached and told me that someone had just donated a new set of the stations. He asked my opinion of them and at what height I thought they should be hung. I had noticed that they were different and was curious about them, as they were very beautiful, and I so loved this new practice that was now a part of my Catholic heritage. He began to tell me about them and then said a very funny thing, "These are not really *new*. They came from the chapel of St. Mary's Villa in Ambler, Pennsylvania. The estate was once used in a movie set. You might have heard of the movie, though it's quite old. It was called *The Trouble with Angels*.

What a tender gesture by my God! Recalling that powerful childhood movement of my soul, I once again welled up with tears. But this time they were tears of joy! My poor pastor, of course, had no idea why I was crying. Something deep, something that had been buried and forgotten about for so many years was, with this one experience, unearthed, polished by His breath of love that had flowed through the words of my pastor, until it shone like a tiny golden nugget, restored to its proper place in my soul. It felt as if my offering of myself to God, which I had thought had been spurned, was now validated. Although my dear pastor could not have grasped what he had said, and why it had such meaning to me, all of the longing that had resided in my heart, the longing that can only be born in the very tender heart of a trusting eight-year-old girl, was finally fulfilled. Some things are just very hard to explain.

As a child, I was unable to go to "take the habit," but God in all of His miraculous weaving of circumstances through divine providence, allowed a bit of the very "convent" from the movie that so touched my heart, to come to me. The Lord, in this one tiny detail, showed me how much He does see, hear, and care about everything!

Each time I walk into Epiphany Catholic Church, round me rings the stations, and I picture the heavenly Father's arms encircling me there. It is like a Holy Kiss, a confirmation from my loving Father God that I have indeed followed the right path. A path that always seems to lead me right back to the heart of Him.

**Praise**: I thank and praise You God that You see, hear, and care about everything, even down to the tiniest details of our lives.

**Prayer:** Dear Lord, thank You for keeping my tears in Your bottle. Thank You for having been my God since before I was born, and for knowing everything about me, even the bits I have forgotten about…but You do not forget. Thank You for being *that kind of God*, the One who sees, loves, understands, and *remembers*. Help me to never forget that about You. Thank You for Your Word that reassures me that You are even more compassionate than a nursing mother, and that You will never forget…You will *never* forget about me. Help me to grow deeper in my faith based on this wonderful knowledge of You. Amen.

**Promise:** "Can a woman forget her infant, so as not to take pity on the child of her womb? But even if she would forget, still I shall never forget you." Isaiah 49:15

**Proof of the Promise:** God longs to heal and restore even the deepest "silly" wounds of our heart. If they hurt us, they hurt Him. He never forgets about us.
**Ponder: Journal here** about any experience that you have had that the Lord "remembered" and answered. Perhaps it was a prayer intention from deep in your past, or a concern that He alleviated unexpectedly, years later. Remember this goodness of the Lord, for it bolsters faith for the future.

## Chapter 11

*"Do not be afraid of Christ! He takes nothing away, and gives you everything. When we give ourselves to Him, we receive a hundredfold in return. Yes, open, open, wide the doors to Christ- and you will find true life." Pope Benedict XVI*

*Life ebbs and flows. Times of troubling discernment can lead to tranquil pools of peace --not the peace of eternity, but rather a foretaste. Not sustainable in this life, but fulfilling nonetheless. In this life of shadows we are privileged every now and again to get a glimpse of the real thing...imparted by the Hand of God and meant to be relished, internalized, and shared...*

**The Nest**

One of the many new and rich traditions I was introduced to as a Catholic was the custom of actually spending time sitting and praying *in* the Church. Since Catholics believe that Christ is "sacramentally and uniquely" present in every Catholic Church, residing in the tabernacle as a consecrated Host, many Catholics choose to pray in the Church, in His Presence, as opposed to praying at home (though it is perfectly acceptable to pray at home, or anywhere at all, for that matter). So that God's people can make a visit, many Catholic Churches stay unlocked all night or at least very late into the night. One of my favorite places to go was, and still is, the upstairs chapel in St. Matthew's Cathedral, Washington DC. I like to sit in the Chapel of the Holy Angels, where I came into the Church. I call it my "Heavenly Nest." It seems quite fitting to take flight up those stairs as my favorite Psalm is Psalm 91 where it states that God "covers us with His feathers" and we "find shelter under His wings" when we "dwell in the secret place" of Him. While sitting there one day, I had an inspiration that when I visited that chapel, I should go and just *be* with Jesus, not bring my laundry list of asks, but instead, just be with Him and sing to Him and love Him from the depths of my being.

One day, while perched in my nest, I began to very quietly sing the song, "Behold the Lamb of God" and as I looked up, I saw a tiny stained glass window with the image of a beautiful little lamb on it. I smiled and my heart welled up with thanksgiving to Him. I then heard Him say these words: "You console My Heart."

I could not believe it! How could *I* console *Him*, the Maker of the World? But somehow, I had. I thought about all of the years of Bible teaching and good works I had done in the name of Jesus. I remembered the mission trips, the lesson plans, the travel and speaking, the weariness with which I fought to do all I felt He had asked me to do—but never in any of these activities did I hear Him say that I consoled Him.

Now, I was merely sitting at His feet, gazing at Him, when I heard Him say those words.

And then again, He came in fullness. I had an impression of being enveloped in a beautiful Light. It was not like before. It was a heavy, weighty feeling of being swallowed up into Light. Yet, it was not just Light—it was an all-consuming, burning embrace of Love. Everything I had ever done wrong was consumed in this Love, like a straw being consumed in a fire. I could not, even for a moment, feel anything but Love. It was so weighty, but in the most miraculous way. It was like "I never wanted to move" sort of a weight. It was as if all of the struggles and works and exhaustions were somehow being pressed out of me. All of the "me" was being consumed by Something so far, far bigger than myself. I could not help but think that no one could ever stand before this LOVE and not be totally consumed by it. There was no fear, as "Perfect Love casts out all fear."[1 John 4:18] There was no guilt, for "he whom the Son has set free, is free indeed…[John 8:36]" And that is exactly what I was experiencing. I could not move for quite some time, nor did I want to. The Light was so joyous! And it brought absolute peace. It had color as well as heat. It was white, then yellow in the center, and radiated out like a rainbow with purple at the very edges, and it danced! Swirling and moving, like a fire that would never burn out. But mostly, above all else, it *loved*. It was *Love* itself, and I never ever wanted it to end.

Of course, it did end, as I am finite and live here where all things are finite. But it made me so look forward to a time when things will be eternal. Love is eternal, but all of the things of this earth will pass away—all the trivial things, all the little mistakes and oopses of our life. All of the misunderstandings, and even the theologies we hold to so tightly, sometimes at the expense of loving our neighbor, and, therefore, at the expense of loving Him—these, too, will pass away. Seeing all earthly things in comparison to this great Love—how insignificant they all seemed. When there is no time, no end, there will be only one thing that matters—how we loved—how we loved Him and how we loved each other. I cannot imagine being separated from this great Love, not even for a moment. The worst words that could ever be heard would be, "Depart from Me, I never knew you."[Matt. 7:23] With even the tiniest taste of this immortal Love, all will forever long to run to our loving God and not from Him in fear. We need only look to the cross to see and experience the deep love He has for us through Jesus Christ.

I saw for the first time how our ruptured Church must grieve Him—this all-Loving Lord—and yet how His great love will even swallow this up, all of our schisms and factions. But for us here, now, division is a painful reality. My own dear family—even we are skewed. We cannot agree on how we will worship and follow God. It breaks my heart, and therefore I am quite sure it breaks His as well. I asked Him about this and this is what I heard, "Your family is a picture of the Church today." I feel like a modern prophet. In the Old Testament, God often used real people and the events of their daily lives as concrete examples, living pictures to portray what was happening spiritually to them. Hosea was one of those "picture prophets." He was told to marry a prostitute to give Israel a visual example of how God was feeling about Israel's faithlessness. Hosea was the picture of fidelity, and Israel was the promiscuous harlot, constantly wandering off chasing after others.

While my family is by no means an apt metaphor, I do feel it sadly portrays the split in the family of God due to theological, cultural, and vocabulary reasons. We are a picture of the Church Universal. And while we do make it work by His grace, it is far less than the ideal of unity He intended and spoke of in John 17:21: "May they all be One, as you, Father, are in me and I in you, that they also may be in us, that the world may believe that you sent me."

I pray that someday we will be one, but until then I ask this: that God give us the faith to believe He is able to do all things, the grace to hope in Him when our own well of hope runs dry and most importantly, that He place in our hearts the love for Him and others that will change our own hearts to be like His—and then to set the world on fire.

Not so many years back, while wandering on the path, groping for clarity in the mists of my journey, I heard this hymn in a tiny Catholic Church in the hills of West Virginia. I was riveted as it verbalized all I felt the Lord was saying to me. It so beautifully expressed my heart's desire to be with Him and "live deeply this new life." I am so thankful for the Catholic Church. I have truly come home to the fullness of the faith through the sacraments and the Church's teachings. I have had a true transformation in my heart, mind, and spirit. I have had a metamorphosis of my soul. I pray that my sharing of my journey (or I should say *our* journey—His and mine—I just rather timidly and sometimes stubbornly cooperated) will, in some way, encourage others who not only want to walk more closely with our Lord, but also want to spread their wings…and fly.

## Hosea
Come back to Me with all your heart. Don't let fear keep us apart.
Trees do bend, though straight and tall, so must we to other's call.
Long have I waited for your coming home to Me and living deeply our new life.
The wilderness will lead you to your heart where I will speak.
Integrity and justice with tenderness, you shall know.
Long have I waited for your coming home to Me and living deeply our new life.

You shall sleep secure with peace;
Faithfulness will be your joy.
Long have I waited for your coming home to Me and
living deeply our new life.

**Praise:** I praise You! You are my Creator—Powerful
and Almighty, yet humble enough to let me console
You.

**Prayer:** Dear Lord, please let me never get so busy
*doing* for You that I forget to just *be* with You, and love
You, and console Your Sacred Heart. I pray that You
will give me the faith, hope, and love I need to follow
You with my whole heart, no matter where that path
may lead, and to love others, even if they do not
follow the same path that I do. Please give me Your
eyes to see the world and Your heart to burn within
me in order to set the world on fire. Lord, please give
me more and more of You, and then the courage that
I need to spread my wings and fly.

**Promise:** "Blessed are those who have been called to
the wedding feast of the Lamb." Revelation 19:9

**Proof of the Promise:** Someday, all that will last or
matter is the way we loved Him and loved each other.

**Ponder: Journal here** about your relationship with
God...Express your heart to Him. If you don't have a
friendship with God, do you desire one? Express that
to Him ( and see *Personal Friendship with God*, Appendix
3),

## Chapter 12

*The Lord sustains all who fall*

*And raises up all who are bowed down. Psalm 145:14*

*When I was little, I remember reading a poster that said, "Please be patient. God isn't finished with me yet." Truer words have never been spoken. In this life, there's always one more lesson to be learned, one more experience to be had, one more chance to love --THANK YOU Jesus!*

## Go Low

One would think that, after experiencing all that the Lord has been so gracious to share with me, I would not struggle as much as I do with the everyday issues of sin. But sadly, I do. It always sneaks in and trips me up in little ways. For example, even if I manage to bridle my rather sharp tongue, I still sometimes have judgmental thoughts. But I have found a great antidote to this problem. Instead of working on "sin management," doing my best to not sin or even think about it, I have discovered it most beneficial to just be with Jesus—to really *be* with Him in the Adoration Chapel, or to look at who He is in His Word and dwell on Him, which makes me want to be more like Him. And if I place myself in the midst of godly people who are like Him, sometimes I hear Him speak to me through them just as clearly as if He was saying things to me directly.

After years and years of teaching the Bible, gleefully explaining the Old and New Testaments via expandable ten foot long wall-charts, timelines, color-coded maps of the Exodus, the divided and restored Kingdoms of Israel, the places that Jesus walked, Paul's multiple journeys in Acts and using scale models of the Tabernacle and the Temple to thrill and engage...I finally got an opportunity to go and see it all, firsthand, for myself. A group of Catholic friends was forming a pilgrimage to the Holy Land and my husband sweetly encouraged me to go as a birthday gift. I shamefully have to admit, I was more than a bit skeptical about taking this maiden voyage with this group, as many Catholics I had met did not seem to know or love Biblical history like I did. My old prejudices were beginning to creep back in. I thought to myself, "I have waited to go and visit the Holy Land all of my life. I want to see and experience it *all*. Will this group know and appreciate what we will see and learn about the Bible? Perhaps I need to go with a group who can deeply appreciate what we will be seeing… some real Biblical experts." Once again, God was shaking His head and laughing at all of my pitiful preconceived ideas and ridiculous judgments.

This, for me, was going to be the trip of a lifetime. This was at the tip-top of my bucket list. I had so longed for this epic adventure my entire life that I had sadly talked myself into the conclusion that *nobody* would be able to produce the trip of my dreams. I reasoned this because I believed I was expecting way too much. Therefore, with a sigh of resignation, I had decided that I should just go on this trip and let God take care of the details. I would go with the modest hope of catching a tiny glimpse of Jesus, and then I would return on a later trip and get all that I might miss this first time-round. Absolute "woe is me" thinking! I embarrassingly confess that, after handing it all over to God, I somehow pridefully believed that not even He could plan a better trip than I could!

But once again, God had something very beautiful in store for me—something I could never have dreamed of. Originally, I was going on this tour as a party of one. At the last minute, however, one of the pilgrims had to cancel and needed a replacement. I had wanted my husband to go, but someone was needed at home to take care of our youngest child. As we were discussing it at the dinner table, my seventeen year old said, "Mom, I would really love to go. If it is at all possible, please take me." I was surprised! She was slated for the varsity lacrosse team at her high school. If she took this trip, which conflicted with spring training, she would automatically be cut from the team . She would have to play at the Junior Varsity level. When I spoke with her about it, she had no hesitation, just a purely joyful spirit and excitement at the possibility of going to the Holy Land so early in her young life. She was to be my new roommate.

The flight was well-organized and uneventful. It was quite late when we finally made it via bus to our beautiful hotel in Haifa. We ended our day with Mass. This was, of course, one of the great perks of the trip. I reminded myself that, if I had gone with just a Bible tour group, Mass at every Holy sight would never have been possible. I was so excited about actually being in the Holy Land that it was difficult to sleep in spite of our long journey. Our first morning, we visited the Church of Stella Mara on Mt. Carmel. This is where Elijah challenged the prophets of Baal to call down fire from heaven on their altars to consume their sacrifices. Of course, God won the contest! It also happened to be where my namesake, St. Therese of Lisieux, derived her order's name, the Carmelites. I also loved St. Theresa of Avila and St. John of the Cross (both Carmelites as well), and so I was greatly humbled to experience the cave where Elijah lived, and to see the humility of the nuns and friars who still live there. It was such a beautiful start to our pilgrimage, and I felt

like St. Therese (both big and small!) and St. John of
the Cross were "picked up" here and all came along to
accompany me.

Our tour guide, who we were just starting to get to
know, was nothing short of genius. He was like a
walking Biblical encyclopedia. And Fr. Donal, the
priest that was with us, just added to the already
spectacular non-stop flow of information, he also had
a deep love and knowledge of the Bible.  And then to
top things off, there was Chris, the trip organizer, who
happened to be a Holy Land fanatic and expert. She
left no detail to chance.  I was beginning to get the
hint— God had planned well for this trip after all-- far,
far better than I could have ever have hoped for...my
silly pride was brought up, right before my eyes and
ears as we were being wowed by all we experienced
from the very first day.

Our next stop was Galilee. Now when I say next stop,
I really mean next little short drive—then stop. I could
not believe how close together everything was. The
diminutive size of Israel was starting to sink in. This is
a place that is only about two hundred ninety miles top
to bottom, and eighty-five miles across at its widest
point. (Compare that to Florida which is four hundred
forty-five miles long and one hundred sixty miles
across at its widest point.) I was stunned. Everywhere
we visited, I realized that, at some point in history,
those people walked. There had been no air-
conditioned motor coach for them. I tried to
remember in scripture if Jesus ever rode a

horse…nope, not that I knew of—only a humble little donkey, the symbol of peace and humility.

When we arrived in Galilee, the only way I can describe how I was feeling was …quite underwhelmed. There was a complete and utter lack of Hollywood spectacle. The remoteness, the sheer human scale and lowliness of it all began to overwhelm me. It was as if the fine white dirt and dust was starting to sink into my soul and take the *shiny* off me. We began to go from town to town (it would have made for a really nice, long jog around the cities on the north end of Sea of Galilee). It was, for lack of a better word…small, and it was surprisingly chock-full of caves. It seemed as though everywhere we went, we would descend several steps (as these sights are very old, and I literally mean, of-biblical-proportions-old) and come to a cave or a *grotto*—a glorified name for a cave. When we finally got to Nazareth (a five to ten-minute drive) there were…caves. Our tour books and signs read "Home of Mary" and "Home of Joseph," but these places sure looked like they were just dug out of the rock—more like caves and rock tunnels than houses. And Nazareth itself is tiny and unglamorous, even today. It seemed to me as though Joseph married the girl in the cave next door. I was so humbled. This is where the Man I admire and love the most was from? I felt as if I had been taken home to meet the family, and had been very surprised. This was not what I was expecting… not at all. This is where the King of the Universe grew up?

Slowly I began to realize, that if I truly wanted to be *like Jesus* I was going to have to have a change of heart...no, more,...nothing short of a total transformation. I was going to need to start thinking, acting, and becoming a great deal more like my meek and gentle Savior if I wanted to be a part of this family. The problem was that I knew that I did not have the capacity to change myself... only He could do it. Jesus reminded me that all I am asked to do is to "humble myself before the Lord," sincerely repent, and ask Him to do the rest. I could cooperate by making my prayer, "Jesus, meek and humble of heart, make my heart like Yours." Funny enough, I was carrying a card with this very phrase on it close to my heart for my friend Karen Goodwin who was very ill. I placed it upon the altar at each holy sight we visited, I would then take my Eucharist for her each day and I could not wait to give it to her when I returned. I took picture after picture of that prayer card at each place we visited so she would feel as if we had all three been on pilgrimage together. That prayer continuously rested next to my heart. I know now that humility is such an attractive and disarming quality when it is genuine. We, of course, saw it in Christ, and now in Pope Francis, and it is really incredibly irresistible. I wanted (and still long to be) like Him, only He can make that happen.

With this newfound desire to be "one of the family," I was now very curious about Jesus and His very humble beginnings, His hometown, and the area where He grew up. Our tour guide was from the region of Galilee, so I felt he spoke with authority and love. He said that, even now, Galilee is "No-wheres-ville."

There is still no university, no industry, and no big cities. When Nathaniel stated in the Gospel of John, "Can anything good come from Nazareth…?"[16] he was obviously familiar with this place! I began to become aware that God was using Jesus' very humble beginnings as a mirror to show me some truths about myself. Ouch!

Each day, as we walked in the steps of Jesus, more and more of His deep and beautiful humility was revealed to me. He walked, literally *walked* this earth. He did not drive a big fancy car. He did not ride in a golden chariot. He was not carried in a sedan chair. He walked. And as He did, He met people right where they were. I can only imagine that the poorest and most humble person would have felt very comfortable with Him. It was the puffed up and proud that would have felt ill at ease. I was beginning to see why.

As I reflected on this environment, I grew more enamored with the idea of humility. It shares its root with the word *human* and the origin is from the Latin root *humus*—earth or soil. "Because *earth* you are, from earth you shall return…" (Genesis 3:19). As we continued on, I was struck and then fascinated by the fact that, try as they may, no one has ever found a single shred of anything Jesus physically left behind in this world (other than the Shroud of Turin, but that was not owned by Him. He was buried in a borrowed grave and "the women" brought the anointing spices and cloth.)  He owned nothing. Nothing. The only things that seem to remain to mark His existence are places they *think* He may have been (and those are based on Byzantine ruins built at least three hundred years after He lived on this earth.) The only things of grandeur that remain in Jerusalem of the era of Jesus are Roman. What a juxtaposition of the WORLD (Rome) versus JESUS. The most influential Man of all times came to earth—to live, and die—and He left not a single mark behind, other than the mark on our hearts and souls, the "seal of the Holy Spirit," (Ephesians 1:13) the eternal marking of His great grace, mercy and love, that forever changed the world.

Every day of this pilgrimage journey was more splendid than the day before. Each day was jam-packed with rich history, stories, geography, and historic holy sights, not to mention Mass at every stop. Jesus met me at every place we visited. He gave me the Grand Tour of Love. We took the "Humble Express" and I heard an echo in my mind of those sweet, chastising words spoken through a smile, "Don't be so quick to judge, Missy."

The pilgrimage concluded in Jerusalem where we spent several days seeing the utterly remarkable "City of God." It was here I learned my most impactful lesson on humility. We visited the Temple Mount and offered prayers at the Wailing Wall (Western Wall of Herod's Temple). Each of us was given an index card on which to write our prayer intentions so we could insert them into the wall. The Jews believe that this is the only portion left of the last Temple (though some dispute this) where God's presence dwelt physically. They believe God's Presence still dwells in these stones even today. It is the most sacred sight in the world for the

Jews. The huge stones were built with "compact unity"—they were hewn off-sight to fit together without mortar and then brought to the Temple mount. I was told that the construction was done in almost total silence. Since this remarkable place has been there for over two thousand years, it is absolutely FULL of little pieces of paper stuffed into the cracks between the stones.

As my daughter and I stood there on the side reserved for the women, taking it all in, I began to see that it was going to be quite difficult to press our requests into the wall. As I am five-foot-two (well, almost), and my daughter much taller than I am, I thought perhaps, if I could drag a chair over close to the wall, she could then stand on it and reach up high, so that we would be assured of a safe place for our prayers. I managed to find a chair and place it right up close to the wall. When I told my daughter the brilliant plan, she sweetly looked at me and said, "I've got this Mama. " At that moment, someone called my name and I turned to answer her. When I turned back to hold the chair for my daughter to climb, I was shocked to see that she was not ON the chair but stooped low, bending down beside it.

She stood up and said, "There! All done! No one thinks to go low! There is lots of room down there!"

"Out of the mouth of babes…!" ( Matthew 21:16) God spoke to me so forcefully in that moment. I had been seeing it all along the pilgrimage in the life of Jesus and now here it was being demonstrated and spoken to me by my daughter... I remembered, "unless you change and become like little children," (Matthew 18:3)... I saw in such a beautiful, humble and natural act of her bending over on hands and knees to serve me out of love that this is what God was asking of me, to "go low" to be willing to bend, to serve, to love, to _____ (fill in the blank!) to do *anything* and do it with a joyful and humble spirit!

I am not sure what the Lord dreams for me next to do, but I do know that whatever it is I have been given a great metaphor for life. It is not the heights we climb, the knowledge we gain, the positions we attain, the wealth we amass or the power we wield that make us great in the eyes of our meek and humble Savior, but the times we stoop, bend, kneel and seek the opportunities to serve those right in front of us, right where He has placed us that make our life worthwhile, that make us more resemble Him. Christ's greatest moment of triumph and glory was that of His voluntary death, the ultimate act of humility, docility to the Father's will, love and service. He became the VOLUNTARY "VICTIM" and because of this, He became the ultimate VICTOR! No one "took His life" He laid it down for us. May we be willing to be transformed to this level..."For greater love has no man than this that he lay down his life for his friends..." (John 15:13) Here's to a life-time of reaching up in praise, honor and imitation of Him by going low in service to others!

**Praise**: Praise you God for showing us the sometimes hidden and little ways to You. "No one thinks to go low!"

**Prayer:** "Loving Lord, I am so humbled when I read about Your majestic heavenly reign and, yet, even more humbled when I look at Your choice of earthly living. You chose to always *go low*. You left the splendor of the courts of heaven to come to earth and to be born, live and die in a cave. You wrote no books, You left no marks except those on the pages of our hearts. I pray, dear sweet humble Lord, that I will be able to 'take up my cross daily' and come after You. I pray that nothing will keep me from You. Not pride. Not doubt. Not fear. No, dear Lord, no-thing. Give me the grace to not fear humility. Make me like You. I want to be Your bride! I throw myself now into Your arms and lay down whatever is keeping me from being One with You. Nothing this earth has to offer could compare to You. Make us One, now and for all eternity."

**Promise:** "So humble yourselves under the mighty hand of God, that he may exalt you in due time." 1 Peter 5:6

**Proof of the Promise:** I have learned that there is always *room*, in every sense of the word, when we are willing to go low.

**Ponder: Journal here** about your hopes and dreams with God… your "spiritual bucket list." Where would you like to be five, ten, twenty years down the road in a spiritual sense? What do you think God's dreams are for you?  Ask Him for the strength, courage and ability to take the next step to get you ...humbly, humbly, humbly...there...by His grace.

# APPENDIX 1

The Catholic Church teaches that Jesus Christ is really present in the Eucharist body and blood, soul and divinity. After the host (wafer) and wine have been consecrated by the priest they change into entirely new substances. This is what is called transubstantiation. We believe this because of what Christ spoke of Himself in the Gospels:
John 6:29-60

> "Jesus answered and said to them, "This is the work of God, that you believe in the one he sent." So they said to him, "What sign can you do, that we may see and believe in you? What can you do?* Our ancestors ate manna in the desert, as it is written;
> 'He gave them bread from heaven to eat.'"
> So Jesus said to them, "Amen, amen, I say to you, it was not Moses who gave the bread from heaven; my Father gives you the true bread from heaven. For the bread of God is that which comes down from heaven and gives life to the world."
>
> So they said to him, "Sir, give us this bread always." Jesus said to them, "I am the bread of life; whoever comes to me will never hunger, and whoever believes in me will never thirst. But I told you that although you have seen [me], you do not believe. Everything that the Father gives me will come to me, and I will not reject anyone who comes to me, because I came down from heaven not to do my own will

but the will of the one who sent me. And this is the will of the one who sent me, that I should not lose anything of what he gave me, but that I should raise it [on] the last day. For this is the will of my Father, that everyone who sees the Son and believes in him may have eternal life, and I shall raise him [on] the last day."

The Jews murmured about him because he said, "I am the bread that came down from heaven," and they said, "Is this not Jesus, the son of Joseph? Do we not know his father and mother? Then how can he say, 'I have come down from heaven'?" Jesus answered and said to them, "Stop murmuring* among yourselves. No one can come to me unless the Father who sent me draw him, and I will raise him on the last day. It is written in the prophets: 'They shall all be taught by God.'

Everyone who listens to my Father and learns from him comes to me. Not that anyone has seen the Father except the one who is from God; he has seen the Father. Amen, amen, I say to you, whoever believes has eternal life. I am the bread of life. Your ancestors ate the manna in the desert, but they died; this is the bread that comes down from heaven so that one may eat it and not die. I am the living bread that came down from heaven; whoever eats this bread will live forever; and the bread that I will give is my flesh for the life of the world."

The Jews quarreled among themselves, saying, "How can this man give us [his] flesh to eat?" Jesus said to them, "Amen, amen, I say to you, unless you eat the flesh of the Son of Man and drink his blood, you do not have life within you. Whoever eats* my flesh and drinks my blood has eternal life, and I will raise him on the last day. For my flesh is true food, and my blood is true drink. Whoever eats my flesh and drinks my blood remains in me and I in him. Just as the living Father sent me and I have life because of the Father, so also the one who feeds on me will have life because of me. This is the bread that came down from heaven. Unlike your ancestors who ate and still died, whoever eats this bread will live forever." These things he said while teaching in the synagogue in Capernaum.

Then many of his disciples who were listening said, "This saying is hard; who can accept it?"

This excerpt is taken from *Mysterium Fidei,* Encyclical of Pope Paul VI, On the Holy Eucharist, September 3, 1965:

"And so Our Savior is present in His humanity not only in His natural manner of existence at the right hand of the Father, but also at the same time in the sacrament of the Eucharist "in a manner of existing that we can hardly express in words but that our minds, illumined

by faith, can come to see as possible to God
and that we must most firmly believe."

## CHRIST PRESENT IN THE EUCHARIST
## THROUGH TRANSUBSTANTIATION

To avoid any misunderstanding of this type of
presence, which goes beyond the laws of nature
and constitutes the greatest miracle of its kind,
we have to listen with docility to the voice of
the teaching and praying Church. Her voice,
which constantly echoes the voice of Christ,
assures us that the way in which Christ
becomes present in this Sacrament is through
the conversion of the whole substance of the
bread into His body and of the whole
substance of the wine into His blood, a unique
and truly wonderful conversion that the
Catholic Church fittingly and properly calls
transubstantiation. As a result of
transubstantiation, the species of bread and
wine undoubtedly take on a new signification
and a new finality, for they are no longer
ordinary bread and wine but instead a sign of
something sacred and a sign of spiritual food;
but they take on this new signification, this new
finality, precisely because they contain a new
"reality" which we can rightly call *ontological*. For
what now lies beneath the aforementioned
species is not what was there before, but
something completely different; and not just in
the estimation of Church belief but in reality,
since once the substance or nature of the bread

and wine has been changed into the body and blood of Christ, nothing remains of the bread and the wine except for the species—beneath which Christ is present whole and entire in His physical "reality," corporeally present, although not in the manner in which bodies are in a place.

Fr. Michael Gilmary, MMA, helps to explain what happens during transubstantiation like this:

> "*Ontology* means the study of *being*. It is based on the Greek word for *being* --- often times you will see icons of Christ where in the nimbus around his head are the words ὁ ὤν .
>
> Those Greek words mean:'the being' or 'the one who is'.
>
> The fundamental point is this: there's a difference in the way things exist: either 'in themselves' as we say, or 'in another'. For example: the table exists 'in itself' or on its own, independent of other things. But does the color in the table exist 'in itself'? Can you find color by itself, existing independent of other things? Can you find a number existing in itself ... meaning, can you find '2' someplace by itself? (Remember, mathematical numbers exist only in our minds, separated or 'abstracted' from matter).

So, things like number, color, etc., exist in other things (they're called the **accidents** of things ... like the shape, weight, taste, etc. of the Eucharist) but the thing that exists as such (or "in itself") we call the **substance** (meaning it 'stands under' = sub - stand).

So, in the Eucharist, the substance changes, but not the accidents."

Christ becomes present in the Eucharist, whether we feel it or not, acknowledge it or not or understand it or not. It is a great Mystery...all we can do is believe in faith and thankfully receive Him there. He longs to give Himself to us in this way where we can truly become unite to Him physically, as one. This is the greatest gift of the Church, for Christ to give Himself to us and then to unite us to Him and one another through it.

*"The cup of blessing that we bless, is it not a participation in the blood of Christ? The bread that we break, is it not a participation in the body of Christ? Because the loaf of bread is one, we, though many, are one body, for we all partake of the one loaf." 1 Corinthians 10 :16-17*

## APPENDIX 2
**Mary, Undoer of Knots**, courtesy of
praymorenovenas.com.

We all have some "knots" in our lives… and Mary can untie them!

The devotion to Mary, Undoer of Knots has become more popular ever since Pope Francis encouraged the devotion in Argentina, and then spoke about it during his first year as pontiff.

The theology of the devotion actually goes back to the second century. Saint Irenaeus wrote that, "The knot of Eve's disobedience was untied by the obedience of Mary; what the virgin Eve bound by her unbelief, the Virgin Mary loosened by her faith."

Mary's faith unties the knot of sin!

Below is a novena that can be prayed to Mary, Undoer of Knots, to seek her intercession for our intentions.

Daily Opening Prayers:

1. Begin each day of the Novena to Mary, Undoer of Knots, with the Sign of the Cross.
2. Make an Act of Contrition. You can use any form; simply ask God to pardon your sins and make a firm purpose of amendment not to commit them again.
3. Optional, but recommended: Pray the first three decades of the Rosary, with the

appropriate mysteries for the day: Joyful (Mondays, Saturdays, Sundays of Advent, and Sundays from Epiphany until Lent), Luminous (Thursdays), Sorrowful (Tuesdays, Fridays, and daily from Ash Wednesday until Easter), Glorious (Wednesdays & Sundays).

4. Make the meditation for the particular day (as follows).
5. Pray Closing Prayers below.

Meditation for the First Day of the Novena to Mary, Undoer of Knots

Dearest Holy Mother, Most Holy Mary, you undo the knots that suffocate your children. Extend your merciful hands to me. I entrust to You today this knot [mention your request here] and all the negative consequences that it provokes in my life. I give you this knot that torments me and makes me unhappy and so impedes me from uniting myself to You and

Your Son Jesus, my Savior. I run to You, Mary, Undoer of Knots, because I trust you and I know that you never despise a sinning child who comes to ask you for help. I believe that you can undo this knot because Jesus grants you everything. I believe that you want to undo this knot because you are my Mother. I believe that You will do this because you love me with eternal love. Thank you, Dear Mother.

Mary, Undoer of Knots, pray for me.

* See Closing Prayers below.

Meditation for the Second Day of the Novena to Mary, Undoer of Knots

Mary, Beloved Mother, channel of all grace, I return to You today my heart, recognizing that I am a sinner in need of your help. Many times I lose the graces you grant me because of my sins of egoism, pride, rancor and my lack of generosity and humility. I turn to You today, Mary, Undoer of knots, for You to ask your Son Jesus to grant me a pure, divested, humble and trusting heart. I will live today practicing these virtues and offering you this as a sign of my love for You. I entrust into Your hands this knot [mention your request here] which keeps me from reflecting the glory of God.

Mary, Undoer of Knots, pray for me.

* See Closing Prayers below.

Meditation for the Third Day of the Novena to Mary, Undoer of Knots
Meditating Mother, Queen of heaven, in whose hands the treasures of the King are found, turn your merciful eyes upon me today. I entrust into your holy hands this knot in my life [mention your request here] and all the rancor and resentment it has caused in me. I ask Your forgiveness, God the Father, for my sin. Help me now to forgive all the persons who consciously or unconsciously provoked this knot. Give me, also, the grace to forgive me for having provoked this knot. Only in this way can You undo it. Before You, dearest Mother, and in the name of Your Son Jesus, my Savior, who has suffered so many offenses, having been granted forgiveness, I now forgive these persons

[mention their names here] and myself, forever. Thank you, Mary, Undoer of Knots for undoing the knot of rancor in my heart and the knot which I now present to you. Amen.

Mary, Undoer of Knots, pray for me.

* See Closing Prayers below.
Meditation for the Fourth Day of the Novena to Mary, Undoer of Knots

Dearest Holy Mother, you are generous with all who seek you, have mercy on me. I entrust into your hands this knot which robs the peace of my heart, paralyzes my soul and keeps me from going to my Lord and serving Him with my life. Undo this knot in my love [mention your request here], O Mother, and ask Jesus to heal my paralytic faith, which gets downhearted with the stones on the road. Along with you, dearest Mother, may I see these stones as friends. Not murmuring against them anymore but giving endless thanks for them, may I smile trustingly in your power.

Mary, Undoer of Knots, pray for me.

* See Closing Prayers below.
Meditation for the Fifth Day of the Novena to Mary, Undoer of Knots

Mother, Undoer of Knots, generous and compassionate, I come to You today to once again entrust this knot [mention your request here] in my life to you and to ask the divine wisdom to undo, under the light of the Holy Spirit, this snarl of problems. No one ever saw you angry; to the contrary, your words were so charged with sweetness that the Holy Spirit was manifested on your lips. Take away from me the bitterness, anger, and hatred which this knot has caused me. Give me, O dearest Mother, some of the sweetness and wisdom that is all silently reflected in your heart. And just as you were present at Pentecost, ask Jesus to send me a new presence of the Holy Spirit at this moment in my life. Holy Spirit, come upon me!

Mary, Undoer of Knots, pray for me.

* See Closing Prayers below.

Meditation for the Sixth Day of the Novena to Mary, Undoer of Knots

Queen of Mercy, I entrust to you this knot in my life [mention your request here] and I ask you to give me a heart that is patient until you undo it. Teach me to persevere in the living word of Jesus, in the Eucharist, the Sacrament of Confession; stay with me and prepare my heart to celebrate with the angels the grace that will be granted to me. Amen! Alleluia!

Mary, Undoer of Knots, pray for me.

* See Closing Prayers below.

Meditation for the Seventh Day of the Novena to Mary, Undoer of Knots

Mother Most Pure, I come to You today to beg you to undo this knot in my life [mention your request here] and free me from the snares of evil. God has granted you great power over all the demons. I renounce all of them today, every connection I have had with them, and I proclaim Jesus as my one and only Lord and Savior. Mary, Undoer of Knots, crush the Evil One's head and destroy the traps he has set for me by this knot. Thank you, dearest Mother. Most Precious Blood of Jesus, free me!

Mary, Undoer of Knots, pray for me.

* See Closing Prayers below.

Meditation for the Eighth Day of the Novena to Mary, Undoer of Knots

Virgin Mother of God, overflowing with mercy, have mercy on your child and undo this knot [mention your request here] in my life. I need your visit to my life, like you visited Elizabeth. Bring me Jesus, bring me the Holy Spirit. Teach me to practice the virtues of courage, joyfulness, humility, and faith, and, like Elizabeth, to be filled with the Holy Spirit. Make me joyfully rest on your bosom, Mary. I consecrate you as my mother, queen, and friend. I give you my heart and everything I have—my home and family, my material and spiritual goods. I am yours forever. Put your heart in me so that I can do everything Jesus tells me.

Mary, Undoer of Knots, pray for me.

* See Closing Prayers below.

Meditation for the Ninth Day of the Novena to Mary, Undoer of Knots

Most Holy Mary, our Advocate, Undoer of Knots, I come today to thank you for undoing this knot in my life.

[Mention your request here]

You know very well the suffering it has caused me. Thank you for coming, Mother, with your long fingers of mercy to dry the tears in my eyes; you receive me in your arms and make it possible for me to receive once again the divine grace. Mary, Undoer of Knots, dearest Mother, I thank you for undoing the knots in my life. Wrap me in your mantle of love, keep me under your protection, enlighten me with your peace! Amen.

Mary, Undoer of Knots, pray for me.

* See Closing Prayers below.

Closing Prayers:

Optional, but recommended: Pray the last two decades of the rosary, with the appropriate mysteries for the day: Joyful, Sorrowful, Glorious.
Pray the Prayer to Mary, Undoer of Knots:
Prayer to Mary, Undoer of Knots

Virgin Mary, Mother of fair love, Mother who never refuses to come to the aid of a child in need, Mother whose hands never cease to serve your beloved children because they are moved by the divine love and immense mercy that exists in your heart, cast your compassionate eyes upon me and see the snarl of knots that exist in my life. You know very well how desperate I am, my pain, and how I am bound by these knots. Mary, Mother to whom God entrusted the undoing of the knots in the lives of his children, I entrust into your hands the ribbon of my life. No one, not even the Evil One himself, can take it away from your precious care. In your hands there is no knot that cannot be undone. Powerful Mother, by your grace and intercessory power with Your Son and My Liberator, Jesus, take into your hands today this knot.

[Mention your request here]

I beg you to undo it for the glory of God, once for all. You are my hope. O my Lady, you are the only consolation God gives me, the fortification of my feeble strength, the enrichment of my destitution, and, with Christ, the freedom from my chains. Hear my plea. Keep me, guide me, protect me, o safe refuge!

Mary, Undoer of Knots, pray for me.
Amen.

Find the Original Here:
http://www.praymorenovenas.com/mary-undoer-knots-novena/#ixzz3SxXz58zx

## APPENDIX 3
Do you have a Personal Friendship with God?

"There is nothing more beautiful than to be surprised by the Gospel, by the encounter with Christ. There is nothing more beautiful than to know Him and to speak to others of our friendship with Him." Pope Benedict XVI

Growing up, I always knew that Jesus loved me and wanted only the best for me and my life. I read this in the scriptures:

"For God so loved the world that he gave his only Son, so that everyone who believes in him might not perish but might have eternal life" John 3:16

(Christ speaking) "I came so that they might have life and have it more abundantly." John 10:10

I also knew that inside of me something was not right. Something was there that caused me to do things that I knew were not pleasing to God. The scriptures called this SIN.

I learned that "sin" is an archery term that means "missing the mark." The Bible tells us that we have all missed the mark in some way, keeping us from intimate union with God Who loves us so much.

*"all have sinned and are deprived of the glory of God." Romans 3:23*

*"For the wages of sin is death... (spiritual separation from God)*
*Romans 6:23*

So how was I to get to the God Who loved me when I knew that it was my sin that kept us apart? God provided a way for me to have my sins wiped clean. His forgiveness provided a reliable pathway.

*"But God proves his love for us in that while we were still sinners Christ died for us." Romans 5:8*

*"For I handed on to you as of first importance what I also received: that Christ died for our sins in accordance with the scriptures, that he was buried; that he was raised on the third day in accordance with the scriptures; that he appeared to Cephas, then to the Twelve." 1 Corinthians 15:3-5.*

*"Jesus said to him, "I am the way and the truth and the life. No one comes to the Father except through me." John 14:6*

*"For our sake he made him to be sin who did not know sin, so that we might become the righteousness of God in him." 2 Corinthians 5:21*

Jesus was the One that took my sin upon Himself and carried it away. He became the way to God, that bridge that closed the gap between us.

I realized that I must believe in Him so that He would do this for me. And I knew that I had to do as Saint John Paul II stated: "Brothers and sisters, do not be afraid to welcome Christ and accept his power....Do not be afraid! Open wide the doors to Christ." I had to open wide the doors of my heart to receive Him.

*"But to those who did accept him he gave power to become children of God, to those who believe in his name," John 1:12*

*"Behold, I stand at the door and knock. If anyone hears my voice and opens the door, [then] I will enter his house and dine with him, and he with me." Revelation 3:20*

How does this happen…? Through prayer.

I prayed a prayer like the one below. Does this prayer express the desire of your heart?

"Lord, I want to have a Friendship with You. I want to know You and Your Love and the things of You. I am sorry for my sins. Please take my sins away and forgive me. Come into my heart and make me the person You always intended for me to be. Help me to live the abundant life You long for me to live with You. Thank You for hearing my prayer. Fill me with Your Spirit and give me your grace, mercy and love… now and forever." I ask this in the name of the Father, the Son and the Holy Spirit. Amen.

As Catholics, we believe that God calls us into a divine love story and His sacraments are like His kisses from heaven-- just for us. In order to live the fullness of the life He calls us to, He has made Himself present: At Baptism it all begins. Confirmation ratifies our calling. The Eucharist fulfills and perfects us. And Confession restores us when we fall shy of the mark. What gifts

He gives us; all of Himself so that we may live fully this blessed life with Him.

Don't be afraid to throw open wide the doors to your heart and walk where Our Lord leads you.
Ask God to fill you more fully today with His Spirit to give you the grace to begin or deepen your friendship now.

If you are feeling called to the Catholic Church, hooray! I have found that it offers the most satisfying feast of LOVE. To get started, you can contact a local pastor, ask a Catholic friend, or contact me directly at www.melissaovermyer.com. I'll be more than happy to point you in the right direction!

*"Convert us to you, that we may be thankful, humble, and devout, for You are our salvation, our courage, and our strength." Venerable Thomas A Kempis*

### Acknowledgements:

I would like to thank with my whole heart

Jesus Christ, who is FULL of Surprises;

Fr. Michael Sliney, LC who God used mightily through his prayers, dogged perseverance, encouragement, and godly example to make all of this possible; Maribeth Harper, my partner in crime, who gave me courage to write, and wind in my wings, with her multi-talented gifts of editing and publishing savvy—and for her years of faithful friendship and deep love of Christ; and Fr. John Pietropaoli, who kindly and patiently read this and reads my blog weekly for error. Someday, I hope to be able to repay him with more than chocolate.

I would also like to thank Karen Goodwin, who believed in me and this journey. Her vote of confidence gave me lead in my pencil. May your beautiful, creative, and loving soul rest in peace.

And thanks to my darling husband, Dale Overmyer, who has always encouraged my every step and given me without hesitation everything I have ever needed to be and do what we felt the Lord was calling *us* to do (as I have always seen the journey and ministries I have been involved in as *our*s.) and my beautiful, faithful, and long-suffering daughters, Emma, Lilly, May, and Daisy, who have put up with me writing and studying, late into the night, speaking when it would have been nice to sit at the dinner table together, and helping me on more than one occasion to "Kick it off at Evermay!" Thank you, girls, for the sacrifices to further the Kingdom! To the Glory of God!

Thanks to my mother, Joan; my father, Frank; my sisters Dede and Marygrace; my grandparents and aunt and uncle; who inspired and formed me, and through whom I first experienced the love of God.

Thanks to my friends, both Catholic and Protestant: Linda, for holding my hand always and for reading and re-reading this multiple times; Heidi, who faithfully prays for me, no matter where my pilgrim's feet may carry me, and who, along with Kathryn and Betsey, masterfully steers the Georgetown Women's Bible Study ship; and Kathryn Lopez, for her friendship and for giving me my "Catholic Voice."

Thanks to my WWP sistas: Lisa (the brilliant!), Julie, Jillian, Krystyna, Maribeth, Marga, Linda, Biz, Ginger, Meghan, Sonja, Anne, Alejandra, Jackie, Catherine, Joan, Glorybell, Judith and all other WWPers who helped to start a fire that will burn into eternity.

Thanks to the Laity Lodge and the Butt-Rogers family who have given so much to so many over the years, especially to my family and me personally. Thank you for the safe place in which to be transformed.

Thanks to my physical therapists Joe and Michael who have helped to keep me upright for all these years!

AND LASTLY, JANICE SMEALIE, WHO INTRODUCED ME TO FR. MICHAEL… SMIRK!

## ABOUT THE AUTHOR

Founder of the Georgetown Women's Bible Study, an Interdenominational Women's Scripture Study Group, I have taught the Bible for over 30 years. I am a convert to Catholicism, and am a part of a group called Catholic Voices, USA, my blog is called something greater. I served on the board of Walking With Purpose Catholic Women's Bible Study. I have been trained to be a part of the Christian Healing Prayer Ministry by Francis MacNutt, and am a member of the Order of St. Luke. I am an artist, author, and speaker. I live in Washington DC with my husband Dale and four lovely daughters.

something greater ministry:
something greater seeks to  serve God by creating opportunities for people to encounter God through prayer, Scripture study, community, and the teachings, traditions and spirituality of the Catholic Church, for the transformation of our daily lives and our world.